We would like to thank all our friends from
Casa Archilei – Centre of Environmental Education
(Fano - Italy), who have encouraged and supported
the project from the beginning, and have welcomed
the 'invasions' of students from several schools.

A big thank you to our families for their
understanding and patience during our countless
Sundays spent working on this project.

Finally, a special thank you to the brilliant editorial
team that made this project available to all our
colleagues around the world.

Damiana and Melanie

© 2006, ELI s.r.l.
P.O. Box 6 – 62019 Recanati – Italy
Tel.: +39 071 750701 – Fax: +39 071 977851
www.elionline.com
e-mail: info@elionline.com

HandsOnLanguage
Green English
by Damiana Covre and Melanie Segal

Graphic design by Studio Cornell sas
Illustrated by Roberto Battistini

Printed in Italy by Tecnostampa – 06.83.191.0

ISBN 10   88-536-1028-X   Green English - Worksheet A
ISBN 13   9788853610287

ISBN 10   88-536-1029-8   Green English - Worksheet B
ISBN 13   9788853610294

ISBN 10   88-536-1030-1   Green English - Special Guide + Audio CD
ISBN 13   9788853610300

Index

HandsOnLanguage

The HandsOnLanguage series offers a wide variety of hands-on activities to be carried out in English. They are all connected to current issues and topics such as the environment, food and nutrition and safety.

A hands-on approach implies that content is learnt via direct experience in an appropriate environment and context so that students are exposed to the language in an authentic manner.

The tasks and the activities that the students have to carry out are designed in such a way that students are stimulated to find out about the environment and to respect it; they learn how to eat properly and how to handle potentially dangerous situations, all starting from observation of reality and experience of it. In this way, students have the opportunity to immerse themselves in the content and the language they are studying (and experiencing), thus becoming more involved in their own learning process.

As a result, teaching and learning does not only happen in the classroom, but also in places which are naturally connected to the topic in question: outside, in the science lab, in the kitchen or in the gym.

The HandOnLanguage projects are structured so as to allow links with other disciplines: from Italian to music, from science to art, from geography to history, via maths and citizenship.

Green English: environmental education, English... and much more!

Green English is an innovative project that combines environmental education with the teaching of the English language to students of school age (from 6 to 11-12).
It is the outcome of an educational programme which started in 1999 in cooperation with the Centro di Educazione Ambientale "Casa Archilei" in Fano (PU), Italy, where over a thousand groups of students have learnt and played with English, nature and science. The worksheets and materials that were tested during these activities have been collected in this publication so that other students, teachers, educators and parents can use them in their own study programmes.

Green English has a double goal: on one hand to encourage students to use English as a real tool for communication to do fun, motivating activities; on the other hand, to promote the development of environmental awareness leading to respect for and appreciation of the natural environment.

Green English provides students with an opportunity to extend their own knowledge and experience connected to ecology and science, while assimilating authentic, spontaneous and coherent linguistic material to store.

The project offers teachers the opportunity of acting in all spheres of learning (intellectual, manual, sensory and affective), stimulating transversal competences (note-taking, observing, classifying, reflecting on cause and effect, hypothesizing) in real situations.

Methodological Approaches

The Common European Framework, the reforms to the education system taking place in many countries all over the world and the substantial changes in a school population which is getting ever more multicultural and heterogeneous in terms of knowledge and ability have, in part, transformed the requirements of schools, teachers and students, posing new challenges and setting new goals.

In general, greater flexibility and personalization of teaching programmes is needed in order to get through to each individual student. The methodological approaches set out in Green English can provide an effective solution to teaching/learning problems and supply an ideal support for approaching the new educational scenario successfully.

THE HUMANISTIC APPROACH
The Humanistic Approach includes a variety of approaches and techniques, such as Georgi Lozanov's Suggestopedia, Caleb Gattegno's Silent Way and Jame Asher's Total Physical Response (TPR). They are all student-centred in the way they address the learning process and the role of the teacher who becomes a sort of facilitator and coordinator of the students' cognitive and affective development.

TASK-BASED LEARNING
In this approach, lesson activities lead towards carrying out a precise task and the language is organized according to the task which the students have to complete.

(CLIL) CONTENT AND LANGUAGE INTEGRATED LEARNING
This approach promotes a type of teaching / learning where language and content are dealt with at the same time in the lesson. This mirrors the child's natural learning process, needing the language to express him/herself to carry out significant actions or tasks. In this way, English ceases to be a "school subject" and becomes a real tool for communication that permits contextualized, authentic and fun activities.

MULTIPLE INTELLIGENCES THEORY / (VAK) VISUAL, AUDITORY, KINAESTHETIC
The theory of Howard Gardner and learning styles, continues to fascinate and win over more and more teachers and educators who recognize its validity, thanks to its success in the classroom and with each individual students.
Green English has activities to stimulate each type of intelligence, including linguistic, logical-mathematical, spatial, inter- intra - personal, bodily-kinaesthetic and musical). In addition, what better opportunity for developing naturalist intelligence could there be than Green English?

LEXICAL APPROACH
Help, there's the past simple! Never fear. Michael Lewis teaches us that structures and lexis can be used as chunks of language (segments of discourse or phrases) that become part of the students' linguistic store because they are necessary in order to carry out a given activity. This methodological approach does not dictate that the linguistic exponents of each worksheet are necessarily analysed on a structural level.
It remains at the teacher's discretion to integrate and further study grammatical and lexical themes that are presented depending on the needs and level of the students.
Students must be simply exposed to the language which will gradually be processed, assimilated and used by the learner when he or she feels ready.

Green English's golden rules and good habits

RESPECT FOR THE ENVIRONMENT – ENCOURAGING RESPONSIBILITY AND INDEPENDENCE
Green English is an environmental education project that equips teachers with strategies to help students form positive values and healthy habits relating to the environment. Green English also helps teachers guide students to personal growth and development from a cognitive and affective point of view, in a relaxed and friendly atmosphere.

LEARN TO SPEAK ENGLISH AT SCHOOL AND AT HOME NATURALLY –
ENHANCING THE MOTHER TONGUE
Using English as the 'official language' of the project can help create team spirit bringing together all the students, as if English were their secret code for communication during Green English time. Day after day, speaking English will become easier, more natural and more fun, even when interacting with other people outside the classroom, interviewing other teachers, students from other classes or family members.
Nevertheless, the mother tongue is not completely banned from the lessons: it could be useful to make students feel comfortable when introducing the project or to better explain unfamiliar topics.
However, switching over from English to the native language and back, should be carefully mediated to prevent the mother tongue taking over English. The teacher may, then, introduce a code-system to allow this transfer such as snapping fingers, whistling, putting on or taking off an accessory and so forth.

GET ORGANISED! – DEVELOPING ORGANIZATIONAL SKILLS
To make the best out of Green English, it is necessary to have the "tools of the trade" to carry out the activities properly and to learn the fine art of organizing. Each student should always have ready:

- Their *Journal* to keep worksheets and all project-related activities together in one place. From past experience, we recommend using a ring binder where A4 plastic pockets can hold the students' work.
- Their *Green English Dictionary*: a notebook (preferably made of recycled paper) where students can write down vocabulary relating to Green English. It really does become a mini dictionary of nature and the environment!
  We suggest using tabs and dividers to separate each letter section, and photocopying the letters from p. XXX of this guide to better identify each single letter of the alphabet and have the students do some enjoyable and creative art work.
- A Clipboard to make note-taking easier while outside or for specific tasks requiring students to move around.
- Stationery: pencils, rubbers, a sharpener, coloured pencils, crayons, glue, scissors, a ruler, and whatever else might be necessary for carrying out individual activities.
- A magnifying glass

RECYCLE
To instil the importance of saving and protecting the environment in our daily lives, students should be encouraged to re-use material that they find at home like: broken pencils, food wrappers, old clothes.

Seasons and Logistics

Green English offers activities for all the seasons that can be carried out in different places depending on the weather, availability and the needs of the class. In general, schools have the use of a garden, which is all that is needed to do a lot of the activities on offer. Many worksheets, however, do not require leaving the classroom and are suitable for use in the winter. In addition, using photographs, nature films, magazines and flashcards can make up for the lack of a real context. We advise, however, organizing the activities outside as much as possible: in a public park, in a house in the country, at a centre for environmental studies, a farm or a garden centre.

Topics in *Green English* A and B

Green English A and B is made up of 10 topic areas with the same topic but with different levels of difficulty in terms of content and language involved.
Every topic area goes into a specific subject through environmental education activities that are backed up by operational worksheets that are designed to be used in a flexible way and not necessarily in order, to meet educational, linguistic and "seasonal" needs of the context in which it is being taught. The teacher can, for example, first look at The Pond (Topic 7) and then Plants (Topic 3) if this is felt to be appropriate to meet the demands of the programme or links with other subjects. The teacher may likewise decide to do some worksheets on a given topic, move on to another and then come back for revision or further study. The back of the worksheets has been deliberately left blank so that it can be used for sketches, drawings, notes, reflections and further activities carried out in the field (where a blank sheet of paper might be necessary), or in class.
To involve students in the project and to encourage group spirit, we advise that topic 1 is always used as a starter:

1. WELCOME TO GREEN ENGLISH
The aim is to form a Green English Team through thinking about some of the basic principles of environmental awareness. Are you ready? Let's go!

Flexibility in the use of the materials still holds, but this is the topic sequence:

2. THE ORCHARD
Everything about trees and their fruit. Classification, measuring and description activities. Observation of the cycle of the seasons and changes in the natural environment (A and B).

3. PLANTS
From the classification of leaves (A) to the photosynthesis process (B) via experiments and field research.

4. THE THREE Rs – Reduce, recycle, reuse
The aim is to sensitize the learners to the problems of garbage. Activities encourage them to think about their own habits related to safeguarding the environment and stimulate their creativity in recycling different materials to build objects and toys (A and B).

5. WATER AND AIR
Water: let's find out about this precious resource through experiments and stories.
Air is a source of life, but what are we breathing? Let's try to keep it clean and help to reduce air pollution (A and B).

6. THE ORGANIC KITCHEN GARDEN
Students are guided towards making their own kitchen garden, in class, in their school or home garden. Activities in plant observation (A), simple suggestions for organic gardening (natural insecticides and fertilizers) and construction of "stick" the scarecrow (B) are also included.

7. THE POND
Towards the discovery of this extraordinary ecosystem: building a mini-pond for observation (A), making food chains (B).

8. BUGS
Hunting for insects in the Green English garden, listening to stories and songs and carrying out observation and classification activities. Suggestions for raising little mascots to look after in class.

9. SEE, SMELL, TOUCH
Nature through the senses – colours, smells, tastes: lots of activities to find out via touching, smelling and listening. (A and B).

10. A HOUSE IN THE COUNTRY
What were our grandparents' houses like? Then, lots of activities: farm animals (A) garden animals, the house today and yesterday (B). And finally, the ecological house where we can save electricity (A and B).

Worksheet Guide

On each worksheet the educator is given information on the aims and principal linguistic exponents and the procedure for carrying out the activity.
The completed worksheets will be kept and can later be put into the Green English Journal or the student's *Portfolio*. Worksheets 1.1 in both levels A and B are designed to be personalized by the student with their own photo, personal information, colours, drawings or decorations and stuck onto the front of the folder as a cover.
The worksheet headers (date, weather) are completed each time and form a habit which introduces the activity. Once the project is finished, the teacher can create a link up with maths to work out weather statistics and temperatures recorded over the length of the *Green English Project*.

Every worksheet is organized in this way:

Topic area title and statement of level (A or B)

WORKSHEET TITLE	Contains the title of the worksheet.
SPECIFIC AIMS	Contains the main linguistic aims connected with the activity (functions-vocabulary-structures).
MATERIALS NEEDED	Contains the list of materials to prepare to carry out the activity.
PROCEDURE	Contains practical information on how to guide the activity. Examples of teacher statements are shown in bold.
FOLLOW-UP	Additional further activities.

To signpost listening activities, reference to or use of Fact Files and Green English Dictionary extension, the following icons have been used:

Green English Dictionary

Audio CD listening

Fact File (FACT FILE)

"Can do" statements

Things I can do ... in English

	a song	a rhyme	a simple story	simple instructions
I can repeat...	(note symbols)	*Incy Wincy Spider...* (spider)	*Once upon a time...*	DRAW

	a fact file	short captions	a simple story	simple instructions
I can understand ...	Fact File	BEES MAKE HONEY (bee/flower)	*Once upon a time*	DRAW

	the parts of a plant	the parts of an insect	material needed	objects
I can label ...	(plant)	(insect)	(paper/pencil)	(scissors/magnifying glass)

"Can do" statements

Things I can do … in English

I can name…

- the parts of a tree
- various kinds of bugs and animals
- substances, equipment and objects

- parts of the body
- different kinds of flowers, trees, plants and herbs
- some fruits and vegetables

I can say…

- the date
- what's the weather like
- my favourite things

- what plants need
- where things are
- what I can do for the environment

"Can do" statements

Things I can do … in English

I can classify…	leaves	insects and animals	living and non–living things	rubbish
I can describe…	a tree / a leaf	a place	the life cycle of …	an insect
I can …				

My favourite Green English activity is:

Student's Evaluation

Student	INTEREST	APPLICATION	AUTONOMY		COMPREHENSION		PARTECIPATION	
	Shows interest in the project	Carries out activities carefully, cooperating with classmates to complete the task.	Asks for explanations about the topics and/or linguistic aspects.	Puts forward ideas, suggestions, solutions, links with other disciplines.	Understands the global meaning of the discourse.	Understands simple questions, instructions and orders.	Participates actively in the conversation.	Answers simple questions. Carries out simple instructions and orders.
1.								
2.								
3.								
4.								
5.								
6.								
7.								
8.								
9.								
10.								
11.								
12.								
13.								
14.								
15.								
16.								
17.								
18.								
19.								
20.								
21.								
22.								
23.								
24.								
25.								
26.								

Yes / No / Sometimes

Teacher's Self-Evaluation

School		Class
Lesson/Activity/Worksheet no.		
Date		

	Description of experience	Suggestions for the future
TIME: Estimated time / actual time spent on activity.		
LOGISTICS Where did the activity take place? Were the settings appropriate/ inappropriate for the activity? Other possible settings/places.		
MATERIALS The materials needed were sufficient, well organized, hard to get...		
LESSON Aspects which worked/ did not work in the lesson: too fast, too slow ...		
ACTIVITY The contents of this activity were sufficient, insufficient, too easy, too difficult, good for motivating students...		
STUDENT PARTICIPATION The students participated/ didn't participate; they helped each other out; they used English to interact with each other/ with the teacher...		
LANGUAGE SKILLS Did the activities help students acquire and/or strengthen their language skills? Which language skills in particular?		
CONTENT ACQUIREMENT Did the activity help students learn (or learn more) about the topic? Which topics?		
COLLABORATION The activities involved other teachers who teach other subjects / from other schools / associations / family members. How were they involved?		

Lesson Planning

Before starting ...

Set your own routines and always have the students:

- write the date on the worksheet
- answer the question *What's the weather like today?*
- tick the daily temperature

This will enable your students to learn about the weather conditions by observing what happens in reality!

This information can be further exploited at the end of the project to make an analysis of how many rainy, sunny, cold, hot days there were during the Green English project.

Students could then create a histogram or pie chart to show the results.

...and now, over to you. Enjoy!

WORKSHEET TITLE	**1.1 Green English Kids**
SPECIFIC AIMS	<u>Communicative functions:</u> asking for and giving personal information. <u>Vocabulary:</u> personal information (**name, surname, age, birthday, address**), natural elements (**animals, berries, flowers, leaves**), various (**colour, favourite, photo, paste, decorate**). <u>Structures:</u> **WH- questions (What, When...).**
MATERIALS NEEDED	A photo of each student, a ring binder with A4 plastic pockets, stationery, glue, seeds, berries, leaves, flowers...
PROCEDURE	1. Ask students to observe the worksheet, concentrate on the words written in the bubble and paste their photos in the box where indicated. **What's a Green English journal?** **Let's make a journal!** 2. Ask students to observe **My Green ID** and to try to understand what information is needed. **Look at the worksheet. What information do we need to complete it?** The students can either complete the worksheets on their own or swap them with other classmates (**Swap your worksheets with a friend**) and complete them. **What's your name?, What's your surname?, What's your address?, How old are you?, When is your birthday?, What's your telephone number?, What's your favourite colour/animal/flower?** 3. Explain to students that this worksheet will become the cover of their journals (the ring binder with the A4 plastic pockets), and that their **Journals** will grow along with them as they collect their completed work. **This is the cover of your Journal.** 4. Ask students to collect/choose some materials to decorate their journal. **Collect some flowers, some leaves and decorate your Journal.**
FOLLOW-UP	Preparing the **Green English Dictionary:** Students cut out the letters of the alphabet from a photocopy of p. 130 of this guide. They paste one letter on a page of a notebook, leaving a few pages in between similar to an address book or A-Z notebook. The children will write and illustrate the words they learn from the activities.

Green English
Environmental Education in English

WORKSHEET TITLE	**1.2 Our Green English Logo**
SPECIFIC AIMS	<u>Communicative functions:</u> following and giving instructions, learning colours. <u>Vocabulary:</u> colours (**red, white, blue, yellow, green, ...**), natural elements (**flower, berry, leaf**), other (**logo, colour, shape, garden, Union Jack**). <u>Structures:</u> **What is it? It's a... What colour is it? Is it ...?** Imperative (**look, find, draw, decorate...**).
MATERIALS NEEDED	Stationary, glue, seeds, berries, leaves, flowers...
PROCEDURE	1. The teacher shows students the Green English Logo. Point out the colours by asking questions about the colours in the logo: **Is it yellow? ...** **Is it blue?** Students identify and write down the colours found in the logo, and they then identify the shape. **Is it a flower? Is it a berry?...** **Tick the right box.** 2. What's inside the logo? The teacher tells the students that the Union Jack, or the United Kingdom flag, is found inside the logo and explain why. **There's the Union Jack on the leaf because we are exploring nature in English.** 3. Ask students to find a leaf and then draw it in the provided space, decorating it in a similar way choosing their own technique. **Let's find a leaf in the garden...** **Draw your leaf here...** As an alternative, students may use the leaf as a "stamp" by dipping it into blue paint and stamping it onto the sheet. Later on, they can draw in the red and white lines of the Union Jack.
FOLLOW-UP 📖 *GREEN ENGLISH DICTIONARY EXTENSION*	Students can start from the beginning and find other materials to design and create a new logo on a sheet of paper, pasting natural objects on it. This project, like the others, can be collected in their **Journal**.

WORKSHEET TITLE	**1.3 Green English Keywords**
SPECIFIC AIMS	<u>Communicative functions:</u> giving and following rules. <u>Vocabulary:</u> keywords relating to positive behaviour and the environment (**respect, reduce, smart, kind, reuse, recycle**), numbers 1-7. <u>Structures:</u> imperative (**Be kind / smart, Respect nature...**).
MATERIALS NEEDED	Stationery, felt-tip pens, scissors, and glue.
PROCEDURE	1. The students cut out the keywords from the first page of the cut outs. **Cut out the words.** The students paste the keywords under the appropriate picture. **Now paste them in the right place.** 2. The teacher asks questions about the pictures using the keywords. **Ex. What's in the picture? What's bad for nature?** **Respect: what?** 3. **KEY:** Boy picking up the bag of crisps = **respect** Recycling bins = **recycle** Adult and child riding a bike = **reduce** Rechargeable batteries = **reuse** Girl feeding a bird = **be kind** Children wearing Green English T-shirts with light bulbs over heads = **be smart** **We should respect nature.** **Look at the bird... let's be kind to little animals.** 4. Students cut out the numbers from the cut out page and paste them onto the worksheet near the keywords, in order of importance for them. Number one is the most important. **Cut out the numbers. What's important for you?** **What is keyword number one for you? And number two?** **Paste the numbers on the worksheet.**
FOLLOW-UP 📖 *GREEN ENGLISH DICTIONARY EXTENSION*	The teacher encourages students to compare their different choices and asks them if any other keywords can be added. **Ex. What's missing in the list?** Make flashcards for positive and negative behaviour relating to the environment.

The Orchard LEVEL A

Green English
Environmental Education in English

WORKSHEET TITLE	**2.1 Parts of a Tree**
SPECIFIC AIMS	<u>Communicative functions:</u> identifying the parts of a tree. <u>Vocabulary:</u> orchard, parts of the tree (**bark, branch, flower, fruit, leaf, leaves, roots, trunk**), colours, parts of the body (**head, body, legs, arms, hands, nose**). <u>Structures:</u> **What's this? It's / This is..., What colour is it? It's...**
MATERIALS NEEDED	**Stationery**
PROCEDURE	1. The teacher explains the meaning of the word orchard. **An orchard is a place with many fruit trees.** This worksheet assumes that it is possible to see the different parts of the tree clearly, preferably in person by planning an outing or by using photos or videos. 2. The teacher asks students to point out their various parts of the body (head, body, legs, arms...) and to observe how trees also have different parts – name them with some descriptions: **This is the trunk.** **It's a very big trunk.** **These are the branches** 3. Ask students to draw each individual part, one at a time. **Draw the trunk** **Draw the roots** **Draw the branches** **Draw the leaves / flowers / fruits...** 4. The students match the names of the parts of the tree with the pictures by drawing arrows. **Match the words with the parts of the tree in your picture.**
FOLLOW-UP 📖 *GREEN ENGLISH DICTIONARY EXTENSION*	Draw the outline of a student on a big piece of paper with his/her arms raised above the head. Transform the silhouette into a tree and make a collage or paint it. At the end, label it with the different parts.

The Orchard LEVEL A

Green English
Environmental Education in English

WORKSHEET TITLE	**2.2 My First Tree**
SPECIFIC AIMS	<u>Communicative functions:</u> describing the characteristics of a tree. <u>Vocabulary:</u> the parts of a tree (**bark, branch, berry, flower, fruit, leaf, leaves, roots, trunk**), colours, characteristics and size (**big, colour, nice, size, small, smell, touch, yucky**). <u>Structures:</u> **It is / it isn't, it has got / it hasn't got.**
MATERIALS NEEDED	Stationery, parts of a tree (leaves, berries, bark, etc.), glue.
PROCEDURE	1. Each student chooses a tree (or a picture of a tree) and copies / draws it on the worksheet. They decorate the trees by pasting on bark, small branches, flowers and leaves. **Choose a tree and draw it here.** **Decorate your tree with bark, flowers and leaves.** 2. The students come together and the teacher helps them fill out the worksheet with questions: **Is your tree big or small?** Use gestures to help students understand. 3. Repeat **It's / it isn't big** or **it's not small** to emphasize the use of the structure. **What colour is your tree? Brown? White?** **Smell it? Is it yucky?** **Has it got leaves and flowers?...** **Has it got fruits?** **Touch it! Is it nice or yucky?**
FOLLOW-UP 📖 *GREEN ENGLISH DICTIONARY EXTENSION* (FACT FILE 3)	The teacher can use the FACT FILE **Different types of Trees** to teach more about the topic.

The Orchard   LEVEL A

Green English
Environmental Education in English

WORSHEET TITLE	**2.3 Seasons**
SPECIFIC AIMS	<u>Communicative functions</u>: talking about typical actions. <u>Vocabulary</u>: natural elements (**beach, flowers, leaves, tree**), seasons (**seasons, autumn, fall, spring, summer, winter**), general vocabulary (**school, birthday, hot, cold**). <u>Language Structures</u>: Present simple (**It is..., it snows, grows, begins...**)
MATERIALS NEEDED	Stationery, flowers, leaves, seeds, twigs...
PROCEDURE	1. The teacher takes the students outside and asks: **What can you see? Can you see leaves on the trees? Why? Because it's (season)...** 2. Students decorate one of the trees according to the season that they are in. **We are in ... (season) so draw a tree in ...** 3. The teacher asks the students to imagine the trees in other seasons and to decorate them accordingly. **What about spring / summer / ...? Decorate the trees in winter, spring, summer, autumn... In spring there are flowers on the tree. In summer there are fruits on the tree. In autumn leaves fall from the tree. In winter there are no leaves on the tree.** 4. The teacher helps students to understand the sentences and asks them to match the sentences to the seasons by writing the correct letter in the boxes: **Write the correct letter in the boxes.** The students try to write other sentences about the seasons.
FOLLOW-UP 📖 *GREEN ENGLISH DICTIONARY EXTENSION*	Students make a collage creating trees in their favourite seasons.

The Orchard   LEVEL A

WORKSHEET TITLE	**2.4 Fruit**
SPECIFIC AIMS	Communicative functions: expressing tastes and preferences, asking about and saying colours. Vocabulary: Fruit (**apples, apricots, blackberries, cherries, grapes, melons, oranges, peaches, pears, plums, strawberries, watermelons**), general vocabulary (**grow, season**), colours. Structures: **Do you like...? Yes, I do - No, I don't; I like... I don't like ... What colour is / are ...?** **It's / They are ...** Plurals.
MATERIALS NEEDED	Stationery, in season fruit.
PROCEDURE	1. The teacher asks a few students: **Do you like pizza? Do you like ice-cream?** The teacher then explains the structure **Yes, I do - No, I don't.** The teacher names various types of fruit (use real fruit if possible, otherwise use the worksheet) and ask students to observe them. **This is an apple. What colour are apples? Do you like apples?** 2. Students draw either a happy or sad face to say whether or not they like the fruits. **Draw a happy face if you like this fruit, draw a sad face if you don't like it.** 3. Students write **I like ... / I don't like ...** next to each type of fruit. 4. Students ask each other questions about the kinds of fruit they like: **Do you like apples / strawberries / watermelons?** Answer: **Yes, I do - No, I don't.**
FOLLOW-UP 📖 *GREEN ENGLISH DICTIONARY EXTENSION* (FACT FILE 18)	Match the fruits to the right seasons and/or months **In January I eat ... / there are ...** using the FACT FILE **Fruit Calendar.** Create a fruit calendar typical of your country.

A

The Orchard   LEVEL A

WORKSHEET TITLE	**2.5 Survey: What's Your Favourite Fruit?**
SPECIFIC AIMS	<u>Communicative functions:</u> asking questions about preferences, understanding simple statistical data. <u>Vocabulary:</u> fruit (see worksheet 2.4). <u>Structures:</u> **What's your favourite fruit? My favourite fruit is... The most popular fruit is...**
MATERIALS NEEDED	Stationery, pictures of fruit, fresh fruit.
PROCEDURE	1. The teacher says: **My favourite fruit is ...,** and then asks students **What's your favourite fruit?** 2. The teacher tells students to write all their classmates' names in the first column of the worksheet. **Write your friends' names in this column.** 3. Tell them to walk around and ask other classmates what his/her favourite fruit is, by writing their names on the worksheet. **Ask your friends: What's your favourite fruit?** 4. Ask them to identify the most popular fruit. **What's the most popular fruit?**
FOLLOW-UP 📖 *GREEN ENGLISH DICTIONARY EXTENSION*	Making a graph (pie, histogram, etc.) that shows the statistics of students' favourite fruits.

Green English
Environmental Education in English

A

WORKSHEET TITLE	**3.1 Growing Things**
SPECIFIC AIMS	<u>Communicative functions:</u> following instructions. <u>Vocabulary:</u> materials for planting (**flower pot, seeds, soil, water**), natural elements (**air, sun**) food (**chocolate, oil, fruit juice**). <u>Structures:</u> imperative (**put, fill, cover, water**).
MATERIALS NEEDED	Plastic flower pots with holes at the bottoms (one for each student or group of students), soil, packets of seeds (ex. **sunflower, beans, zinnias**), water. Other materials which are not necessary for planting and growing plants (ex. **a packet of sugar, a ruler, etc**).
PROCEDURE	1. The teacher shows students various materials and asks them to guess which ones are necessary for sowing. **Do we need sugar to plant a seed? Do we need a ruler? No, of course we don't.** **Do we need a flower pot? Yes!** 2. After identifying the materials needed for planting, ask students to draw pictures of them in the right box. **Draw a flower pot in the right box.** 3. The teacher asks students to guess what they need to do. **What do we do first? And then?** 4. The students fill in the gaps in the instructions. **KEY:** Fill the **POT** with **SOIL** Put the **SEED** in the **SOIL** Cover the **SEED** with **SOIL** 5. Students now plant their seeds. 6. Talking about what the plant needs in order to grow. **Do you think plants need fruit juice?** **Does your plant need chocolate?** Students then choose which elements (**sun, water, air**) are necessary for the plant and they draw them.
FOLLOW-UP 📖 *GREEN ENGLISH DICTIONARY EXTENSION*	Survey: what plants have you got at home? **How many plants have you got at home? Where are they?** **Are they big or small plants? Have they got flowers?**

WORKSHEET TITLE	**3.2 What Do Plants Need?**
SPECIFIC AIMS	<u>Communicative functions:</u> giving and following instructions, describing the evolution of a phenomenon. <u>Vocabulary:</u> objects (**cupboard, flower pot, fridge, shoe box, window sill**), natural elements (**bean seeds, cress seeds, plant, soil, water**), expressions of time (**day, week**). <u>Structures:</u> Imperative (**put, water, observe**), **What ...? Where...?**
MATERIALS NEEDED	5 flowers pots, soil, cress or bean seeds, shoe box, water, fridge, cold environment.
PROCEDURE	1. The students draw the materials needed for the activity and plant the seeds (see worksheet 3.1) **Put the seeds in the pots with soil.** 2. The students read the instructions and try to understand where they must put the plants. **Where shall we put the plants? Where is the window sill?** 3. The class observes over time the plant's growth and completes the observation table with simple sentences. **There is no plant. The plant has got ... leaves. The leaves are yellow. ...**
FOLLOW-UP 📖 *GREEN ENGLISH DICTIONARY EXTENSION*	Talking about what are the best conditions for a plant to grow in. **Where do plants grow best?** Look in some books or on the internet for some photos of plants in poor conditions (wind that has bent them over, rocks that block the roots, little light, lack of water...)

Green English
Environmental Education in English

A

WORKSHEET TITLE	3.3 Leaf Rubbing
SPECIFIC AIMS	<u>Communicative functions</u>: giving and following instructions. <u>Vocabulary</u>: stationery (**crayons, glue, paper, paste, scissors, sheet**), general vocabulary (**garden, leaf, decoration**). <u>Structures</u>: imperative (**collect, put, rub, cut out, label, use**).
MATERIALS NEEDED	Different kinds of leaves in terms of consistency, shape and size, paper, scissors, glue, pencils or crayons.
PROCEDURE	1. The teacher takes the students outside to collect some leaves (or can bring some leaves to the classroom - thick leaves work best like oak, bay, maple leaves...). **Let's collect some leaves. Today we are doing leaf rubbing.** **Choose your favourite leaf. We have big hard leaves and small soft leaves...** 2. The teacher shows the students the materials that are needed for the activity and asks them to draw them in the boxes. **Draw a pair of scissors.** The teacher then asks them to find the odd one out (**glue**) and to then draw the materials that are necessary for the activity (**pastels, crayons...**). 3. The teacher gives the instructions and the students carry out the different steps for leaf rubbing: **Put the leaf under the paper.** **Rub the crayon all over the sheet of paper with your favourite colour.** **What can we do with these beautiful leaves?** **...**
FOLLOW-UP 📖 *GREEN ENGLISH DICTIONARY EXTENSION* (FACT FILE 15)	Making a poster with the names of the different kinds of leaves using FACT FILE Leaf Rubbing. Create a collage with dry leaves.

WORKSHEET TITLE	**3.4 Leaf Classification**
SPECIFIC AIMS	<u>Communicative functions:</u> classifying leaves based on their characteristics, expressing size, describing natural elements. <u>Vocabulary:</u> related to the sense of touch and characteristics of a leaf (**big, compound, margin, entire, hairy, hard, heart-shaped, lance-shaped, length, lobed, oval, prickly, shape, simple, slender, small, soft, toothed, wide, width**). <u>Structures:</u> **What is ... like? It's ...** Imperative (**measure**).
MATERIALS NEEDED [FACT FILE 16]	Leaves, stationery, ruler (for measuring), FACT FILE Leaf Classification.
PROCEDURE	1. The teacher takes the students outside to collect some leaves (or brings some leaves to the classroom). **Let's collect some leaves/Look at these leaves.** 2. The teacher explains and shows the characteristics of a leaf • size • what it feels like to the touch • shape • margin • structure (simple or compound) 3. The students draw the different leaves in the boxes based on their characteristics. **Draw the different leaves in the boxes. A small leaf here..., Ouch, this leaf is prickly... Where do we draw a prickly leaf?** 4. The students choose their favourite leaf and describe it. **This leaf is very strong. It's prickly and lance-shaped. It's simple and it's 5 cm long.**
FOLLOW-UP 📖 *GREEN ENGLISH DICTIONARY EXTENSION* [FACT FILE 16]	Students can make a herbarium and dry leaves in it. They then write a detailed description of it. The leaves can be left to dry in books with paper towels, or wrapped up in paper towels in the microwave oven for a few seconds held firm in between two ceramic plates pressed together.

WORKSHEET TITLE	**4.1 Survey (1) What Do You Recycle?**
SPECIFIC AIMS	<u>Communicative functions</u>: interviewing (asking for information) <u>Vocabulary</u>: related to recycling (**aluminium, glass, organic, waste, paper, plastic, recycle**). <u>Structures</u>: **What ...?** Present simple question form (**Do you recycle...?**)
MATERIALS NEEDED	Pencil, paper, plastic bottle, glass bottle, tin can, banana peel or another type of organic waste, photo of rubbish tip.
PROCEDURE	1. The teacher shows students all the objects and tells them what materials they are made of. **This is plastic... and this is glass.** **This is aluminium... and this is paper.** **What's this? This is organic waste.** 2. One student goes out of the classroom. One object is removed from the table. When the student comes back, the teacher asks: **What's missing?** (This is a good opportunity for the teacher to teach the dialogue: **[knock, knock] Can I come in?**). 3. The teacher explains to the students that the recycling symbol (three green arrows) represents a "cycle." Then the teacher introduces the problem of waste by showing them photos or by having them carry out a research on why it is necessary to recycle. **This is the symbol of recycling. There is too much rubbish!** **Recycling is very important!** 4. The teacher asks students what they recycle and asks them to colour in the first row of boxes with the right colour. **I recycle paper and plastic. What do you recycle? Colour the boxes.** 5. Students write down their classmates' names and continue with the worksheet by asking them what they recycle at home. **Write your friends' names here.** **Now ask your friends what they recycle.** **What do you recycle? Do you recycle glass?**
FOLLOW-UP 📖 *GREEN ENGLISH DICTIONARY EXTENSION*	**Worksheet 4.2 - Survey 2** **Waste Hunt: What's in the rubbish bin?** Students observe and take notes of what is thrown away at home / in the classroom over a certain period of time.

The Three Rs LEVEL A

Green English
Environmental Education in English

WORKSHEET TITLE	4.2 Survey (2) How Much Do You Recycle?
SPECIFIC AIMS	<u>Communicative functions:</u> asking about quantity. <u>Vocabulary:</u> related to recycling (**aluminium, glass, organic waste, paper, plastic, recycle**), numbers. <u>Structures:</u> **How many ...?, How much ...?**
MATERIALS NEEDED	Stationery.
PROCEDURE	1. The teacher asks students to complete the graph using the data from worksheet 4.1. **Now let's take the data from your survey and complete this graph.** 2. Students calculate the number of students who recycle the different materials, answer the questions at the bottom of the worksheet and comment on the results. **How many children recycle... paper?** **In our class ... children recycle paper but nobody recycles organic waste.** 3. The teacher asks students to think about how much and what they recycle, and then encourages them to think about it. **How much do you recycle?**
FOLLOW-UP 📖 *GREEN ENGLISH DICTIONARY EXTENSION*	Interview other teachers and / or family members and friends: **How much do you recycle?** **What do you recycle?**

The Three Rs   LEVEL A

Green English
Environmental Education in English

WORSHEET TITLE	**4.3 Rubbish Bins**
SPECIFIC AIMS	<u>Communicative functions:</u> classifying objects according to material. <u>Vocabulary:</u> recyclable materials and objects (**aluminium, bin, cardboard, glass, organic waste, paper, plastic, rubbish**). <u>Structures:</u> **What's made of ...?**
MATERIALS NEEDED	Stationary, various objects: plastic bottles, glass bottles, apple core/banana or orange skin, cardboard/paper (newspaper, cereal box etc ...), tins etc... 6 large boxes or plastic bins like the ones used for paint.
PROCEDURE	1. Students complete the words using the illustrations to help them. To make the activity easier, the teacher could write the letters that are needed to complete the words in random order on the board. **Fill in the blanks and complete the words.** **Look at the pictures.** **Key:** **PLASTIC , ORGANIC WASTE, ALUMINIUM, PAPER, GLASS** 2. The teacher asks **"What's made of plastic? What's made of glass?** The students match each type of rubbish to its bin. **Match the pictures to the bin.** Students draw various objects in the bins depending on what material they're made of . **Draw some plastic bottles/some glass bottles/ some aluminium cars/an orange skin in the right bin.** 3. The teacher divides the class into 6 groups and asks them to decorate 6 large boxes or bins with their pictures to make containers for separate rubbish collection. **Now use your drawings to decorate the bins.** NB: Some local councils have compost bins outside for recycling organic rubbish. Students enjoy observing them crawling with the animal life that grows there over a few weeks.
FOLLOW-UP 📖 *GREEN ENGLISH DICTIONARY EXTENSION*	Make a map of all the recycling points where recycling can be taken in the area. **Let's draw a Recycling Map.**

The Three Rs   LEVEL A

Green English
Environmental Education in English

Worksheet Title	**4.4 Reuse: Let's Make a Puppet**
Specific Aims	<u>Communicative functions:</u> following instructions. <u>Vocabulary:</u> parts of the body (**arms, ears, eyes, head, legs, mouth, neck, nose**), various materials and objects (**plastic bottle, cardboard, cloth, puppet, scissors, stapler, sticky tape, top, wool**). <u>Structures:</u> imperative (**cut, make, draw, stick, screw, unscrew, staple, fix**).
Materials Needed	Stationery, scissors, sticky tape, stapler, cardboard from reusable material (ex. packet of rice, box of cereal...), leftover cloth, plastic bottle, leftover wool.
Procedure	1. The teacher shows the students the materials in a random order and asks them to draw the objects in the right boxes. **What is this? Draw it in the right box.** 2. The teacher says: **Today we are going to recycle all these materials and make ... a puppet.** Following the instructions one or more puppets are made, depending on how much material there is. 3. The students fill in the instructions with the missing words and make the puppet. **KEY:** **1. bottle** **2. head** **3. mouth, eyes, ears, nose** **5. head** **6. top** **7. neck** **8. top** **10. arms, legs**
Follow-Up 📖 *Green English Dictionary Extension*	Have a puppet show using the puppets that students made. In groups, the students make an object out of reusable material. They can also make them at home. Students can set up an exhibit, market, or contest to show them off.

WORKSHEET TITLE	**4.5 Make Your Own Paper**
SPECIFIC AIMS	<u>Communicative functions:</u> following instructions. <u>Vocabulary:</u> various objects, materials, natural elements (**paper, bucket, water, blender, cloth, plastic bowl, flowers, seeds, leaves, nylon stocking, clothes hanger**). <u>Structures:</u> imperative (**let's make, tear, put, leave, blend, fill, dip, cover, turn**), prepositions (**in, into, with, over, for**).
MATERIALS NEEDED	Stationery, recycled paper (printer paper or notebook paper work best - the paper will come out greyish if newspapers are used), bucket, water, blender, cloth, plastic bowl, sieve made with a metal clothes hanger and nylon stockings. Optional: dried flowers, little seeds, leaves.
PROCEDURE	1. The teacher shows the materials in random order and asks students to draw them in the boxes. **This is a bucket. Draw a bucket in the box.** 2. The students observe the pictures and make the recycled paper following the teacher's instructions. **Let's make recycled paper!** **Tear the paper into small pieces.** **Put the pieces of paper in a bucket with water.** **Leave for an hour.** **Fill the blender with water and paper.** **Blend.** **Fill the plastic bowl with the pulp. You can add seeds, flowers and leaves.** **Use a clothes hanger to make a frame.** **Cover it with a nylon stocking.** **Dip the frame in the bowl and pick up some pulp.** **Cover the frame with a piece of cloth.** **Turn the frame over and put the cloth in the sun to dry.** 3. Students draw the sun in the last box. **And now ... Draw the sun and let it dry.**
FOLLOW-UP 📖 *GREEN ENGLISH DICTIONARY EXTENSION*	When the paper is dry, the students can make cards, the cover of a notebook, a collage and many other creative things.

Green English
Environmental Education in English

WORKSHEET TITLE	**5.1 Soluble/ Insoluble**
SPECIFIC AIMS	<u>Communicative functions:</u> following instructions, expressing countable and uncountable quantities, expressing facts. <u>Vocabulary:</u> food (**water, sugar, salt, oil**), objects (**sand, stones, glass, spoon**), adjectives (**soluble, insoluble**). <u>Strutture:</u> present simple, imperative (**put, wait, stir**), quantifiers (**some**).
MATERIALS NEEDED	Stationery, water, 5 transparent plastic glasses and 5 small spoons for each group, sugar, oil, salt, stones, sand.
PROCEDURE	1. The teacher shows students the materials and they draw them in the boxes: **Draw some sugar, draw some oil, ...** 2. Ask the students to match the pictures with the sentences, writing the letter in the correct box. **Match the sentences with the pictures...** **Sentence number one is ...? Right, 'put the water in the glasses' is A, and then? Okay, number two is B.** **KEY:** **1A, 2B, 3D, 4F, 5E, 6C, 7G.** 3. The teacher splits the class into groups and asks them to follow the steps of the previous exercise. **Now, put the water in the glasses. Put some sugar in one glass. Put some oil in another glass. Etc...** 4. The teacher asks the students to observe the five glasses and answer yes or no. **Now have a look at the glasses... What can you see? Does oil disappear? No, it doesn't...** **And salt? Can you see it? It disappears!** 5. The teacher reads the two descriptions soluble / insoluble and asks the students to complete the conclusions. **Sugar disappears. So sugar is ...? Yes, sugar is SOLUBLE.**
FOLLOW-UP 📖 *GREEN ENGLISH DICTIONARY EXTENSION*	Do experiments with other substances chosen by the students (ink, paint, sponges, metal...).

Green English
Environmental Education in English

A

WORKSHEET TITLE	**5.2 Does It Float?**
SPECIFIC AIMS	<u>Communicative functions:</u> following instructions, asking questions and making conclusions. <u>Vocabulary:</u> various objects (**leaf, paper, paper clip, stick, stone, water**). <u>Structures:</u> **What ...? present simple (floats / doesn't float).**
MATERIALS NEEDED	Stationery, stone, leaf, stick, paper clip, paper, a bowl to contain water.
PROCEDURE	1. The teacher asks students to match the objects to their names and to follow the instructions. **Match the objects to their names and follow the instructions.** 2. The students carry out the experiment. **Put the stone in the water...** **Put the paper clip in the water...** 3. The teacher asks students to complete the worksheet using floats / doesn't float. **What happens to the stone? Does it float?** **Yes, it does / it floats.** **No, it doesn't / it doesn't float.** 4. Repeat the experiment with other objects.
FOLLOW-UP 📖 *GREEN ENGLISH DICTIONARY EXTENSION*	A field trip to a pond: students throw a stone, a leaf, a stick or other natural objects and observe what happens. Then, they can make a poster with *it floats / it doesn't float* to record this experience.

WORKSHEET TITLE	🎧 **5.3 Drip the Drop**
SPECIFIC AIMS	<u>Communicative functions:</u> understanding facts told in a sequence. <u>Vocabulary:</u> natural elements (**water, drop, sea, sun, sky, cloud, rain, river**). <u>Structures:</u> Present simple for story-telling.
MATERIALS NEEDED	Stationery, pictures (from magazines) of: drops of water, the sea, clouds, the sky, the sun, rain, a river.
PROCEDURE	1. The teacher plays the story Drip the Drop (GREEN ENGLISH AUDIO CD, TRACK 2), encouraging students to follow the story looking at the pictures from the worksheet. 2. The teacher asks students to draw the missing pictures. **Draw the missing pictures.** 3. The teacher starts the story over again emphasizing the cyclic nature of the story on the worksheet. At the end the teacher asks: **And now? Where is Drip?** 4. The teacher asks students to act out the story by miming it in order (a sentence each).
FOLLOW-UP 📖 GREEN ENGLISH DICTIONARY EXTENSION	Invent, draw or act out Drip's adventures (ex. what Drip sees in the river, if he is scared, who he meets, what happens in winter).

WORKSHEET TITLE	5.4 Survey: How Do You Go to School?
SPECIFIC AIMS	<u>Communicative functions</u>: talking about means of transport. <u>Vocabulary</u>: means of transport (**bike, bus, car, foot**), numbers. <u>Structures</u>: **How ...? How many ...? By + means of transports, on foot.**
MATERIALS NEEDED	Stationery, pictures of different types of transport.
PROCEDURE	1. The teacher says: **I come to school by bike. And you? How do you come to school?** 2. The teacher asks students to complete the chart by doing a survey with their classmates. **Ask your friends how they come to school and fill out the chart.** 3. The teacher asks the students to answer the questions at the bottom of the worksheet. **How many children go to school by bike?** **How many children go to school by bus?** **How many children got to school by car?** **How many children go to school on foot?**
FOLLOW-UP 📖 *GREEN ENGLISH DICTIONARY EXTENSION*	Make a graph (histogram, pie...) that shows the results of the survey. Interview other teachers, family members, friends.

Water and Air LEVEL A

Green English
Environmental Education in English

WORKSHEET TITLE	5.5 Transport Record
SPECIFIC AIMS	Communicative functions: talking about past actions, talking about frequency of actions. Vocabulary: means of transport (**car, bike, train, bus**), days of the week (**Monday, Tuesday, Wednesday, Thursday, Friday, Saturday, Sunday**), adverbs of frequency (**never, sometimes, usually, often, always**). Structures: **How often ...?, On + day**, Past simple (**go / went, come / came, walk / walked**), adverbs of frequency (**never, sometimes, usually, always**).
MATERIALS NEEDED	Stationery, pictures of different kinds of transport.
PROCEDURE	1. The teacher asks the students to record the means of transport that they use during the week. **Let's keep a record of the means of transport we use weekly.** 2. The teacher asks students to complete the sentences: **On Monday I went to school by car, and you? Write it.** **On Tuesday I went to the swimming pool by bus...** 3. The teacher then shows the rate of frequency with the adverbs and asks students to make sentences like the examples. **How often do you walk to school?** **How often do you go to school by bus?** **Complete the sentence: I never... / I usually ...**
FOLLOW-UP 📖 *GREEN ENGLISH DICTIONARY EXTENSION*	Interview family members / other teachers and write it down in the Journal. **How does your mum / Mr /Mrs ... go to work?** **And your Dad / Mr / Mrs...?**

WORKSHEET TITLE	**6.1 Organic Vegetables**
SPECIFIC AIMS	<u>Communicative functions:</u> identifying and describing vegetables. <u>Vocabulary:</u> vegetables (**asparagus, cauliflower, celery, peas, beans, carrots, potatoes, garlic, artichoke, onion, pumpkin, lettuce, courgettes, sweet pepper, aubergine...**), colours (**red, yellow, orange, white, green**). <u>Structures:</u> **It's ..., They are ...**
MATERIALS NEEDED	Stationary, vegetables or pictures of vegetables, a bottle of pesticide for plants.
PROCEDURE	1. The teacher writes on the board: **ORGANIC: A very important word!** The teacher asks the students to guess what the word means and helps them by showing the bottle of pesticides: **Why is this word important? What does it mean? Is it a good word or a bad word?** The teacher helps students to reach the following conclusion: **An organic kitchen garden is special: there are no chemicals and pesticides.** 2. The teacher describes the various types of vegetables and asks students to guess what vegetables they are: **They are orange, long and sweet.** **Yes! Carrots!** 3. The teacher asks the students to cut out the names of the vegetables from the cut out page. Students paste the names under the right vegetable. **Now cut out the names of the vegetables and paste them on your worksheet.** **KEY:** **garlic, cauliflower, artichoke / asparagus, carrots, courgettes / pumpkin, onion, sweet pepper / beans, potatoes, celery / lettuce, peas, aubergine.**
FOLLOW-UP *GREEN ENGLISH DICTIONARY EXTENSION*	**GUESSING GAME.** Students are blindfolded and take turns guessing what vegetable it is by the smell and taste of it. **PICTIONARY.** One student draws a part of a vegetable on the blackboard and the others have to guess what it is. If they don't guess it, the student continues to draw the rest of the vegetable until the others guess it.

The Organic Kitchen Garden LEVEL A

Green English
Environmental Education in English

WORKSHEET TITLE	**6.2 Survey: What's Your Favourite Vegetable?**
SPECIFIC AIMS	<u>Communicative functions</u>: asking about and talking about favourite vegetables, numbers and quantities. <u>Vocabulary:</u> vegetables (teacher's choice, some examples: **asparagus, cauliflower, celery, peas, beans, carrots, potato, garlic, artichoke, onion, aubergine, tomato, pumpkin, lettuce, courgettes, sweet pepper**). <u>Structures</u>: **What's your favourite vegetable? / My favourite vegetable is.../ The most popular vegetable is ...**
MATERIALS NEEDED	Stationery, pictures of vegetables if it is not possible to go to a kitchen garden.
PROCEDURE	1. Visit a kitchen garden, if possible, and observe the different kinds of vegetables present. **This is a kitchen garden.** **What vegetables can you see?** **Yes, lettuce... And then? onions, of course!** 2. The students write their classmates' names in the column. **Now write everybody's name in the boxes.** 3. Students observe the vegetables in the kitchen garden or in the photos. They write down what their favourite vegetable is and ask their classmates what their favourite vegetables are, writing down their names on the worksheet. **What's your favourite vegetable?** **My favourite vegetable is...** **Ok, Paolo's favourite vegetable is...** 4. The teacher asks about all the vegetables. **How many children like cauliflower? Seven? Good!** 5. The students write down which vegetable is the most popular. **Which is the most popular vegetable? Lettuce? Good!** **Write it on your worksheet.**
FOLLOW-UP 📖 *GREEN ENGLISH DICTIONARY EXTENSION*	Students interview (in English) family members, neighbours and other teachers.

WORKSHEET TITLE	🎧 6.3 Song: This Is the Way
SPECIFIC AIMS	<u>Communicative functions:</u> describing actions. <u>Vocabulary:</u> nouns related to the kitchen garden (**kitchen garden, ground, seeds, plants, veggies**). <u>Structures:</u> present simple (**weed, dig, plant, water, feed, grow, eat**), **this is...**
MATERIALS NEEDED	Stationery, gardening tools, compost, an area in a garden (and/or pictures and drawings of the actions).
PROCEDURE	1. The teacher brings the students (if it's possible) to the area set up for creating a kitchen garden. **Here we are in our kitchen garden...** **Today we'll prepare our kitchen garden... look at me and listen!** 2. The teacher says, or sings, the actions of the song (**get rid of the weeds, dig, plant the seeds, water it, spread the compost**) and carries them out. The teacher also mimes a plant **growing** and pretends to **eat** some vegetables...), and asks students to do the same. **Come on, let's weed the garden!** 3. The teacher plays the song (GREEN ENGLISH AUDIO CD - TRACK 3). **This is the way...** The music without words on Track 4 can be used for singing with the students. 4. The students draw the actions of the song after having worked in the kitchen garden. **Now you can draw in the boxes... what's 'weed the garden?' Do you remember?**
FOLLOW-UP 📖 *GREEN ENGLISH DICTIONARY EXTENSION*	SIMON SAYS is an action game. The students do the actions only when the teacher or another student calls them out with 'Simon Says' before the action. Whoever makes a mistake is out of the game. Make a poster with pictures or captions of students in the kitchen garden (it can also be used for an exhibit).

WORKSHEET TITLE	**6.4 In the Kitchen Garden**
SPECIFIC AIMS	<u>Communicative functions:</u> expressing favourite foods, identifying parts of vegetables. <u>Vocabulary:</u> vegetables (**cauliflower, celery, peas, beans, carrot, potato, garlic, artichoke, onion, aubergine, courgette, sweet pepper...**) parts of a plant (**leaves, stem, roots, fruit, flower, bulb, seeds, tuber...**) <u>Structures:</u> **Is there...? Is it...? / Do you like ...?** present simple (**eat**).
MATERIALS NEEDED	Stationery, kitchen garden (or pictures).
PROCEDURE	1. The teacher brings the students to the kitchen garden or shows the pictures and asks them to identify the various vegetables. **Look around and tell me ... What vegetables can you see? What is this?** 2. The students put a tick or a cross on the worksheet to indicate whether or not they see the vegetables. They also fill in a happy or sad face based on their preferences. **Tick here if you can see artichokes, or cross if you cannot see them... Do you like artichokes? Yes? Good! Draw a happy face! / No? Oh! Draw a sad face.** 3. The teacher asks them what parts of a plant are edible. **Which part do you eat? Yes, good! The flower!** **What about courgettes? Which part do we eat? The fruit, sure!** **KEY:** **Artichoke / flower** **courgette / fruit and flower** **beans / seeds** **carrot / roots** **cauliflower / flower** **celery / stem** **aubergine / fruit** **garlic / bulb** **lettuce / leaves** **onion / bulb** **peas / seeds** **potato / tuber** **sweet pepper / fruit** 4. The students write down the parts that we can eat.
FOLLOW-UP *GREEN ENGLISH DICTIONARY EXTENSION*	The students take notes in English of the vegetables they've eaten at home and at the school canteen for a week.

The Pond LEVEL A

WORKSHEET TITLE	**7.1 In and around the Pond**
SPECIFIC AIMS	<u>Communicative functions:</u> describing places, finding objects. <u>Vocabulary:</u> prepositions of place (**in, under, on, over, around**), vocabulary related to the pond (**water, frog, dragonfly, fish, duck, water lily, turtle, aquatic plants, worm, ground, rocks**). <u>Structures:</u> **Is there …? Are there …?, There is / There isn't …, There are / There aren't … + short answers.**
MATERIALS NEEDED	A pond to observe.
PROCEDURE	1. The teacher brings the student to a pond and asks them to find some living creatures and other typical elements that can be found around a pond. **This is a pond.** **Observe the pond and find something special.** **Are there any animals? Any plants or flowers?** 2. The students observe the illustrations of the pond for one minute. They then turn the page and answer the teacher's questions. The teacher uses gestures to introduce the prepositions of place. **Is there an elephant in the pond?** **Is there a frog on a leaf?** **Is there a dragonfly in the air?** **Is the fish on the ground? No? Good! Where is it?** **Excellent! Under a water lily.** 3. The students complete the sentences with prepositions. **KEY:** **dragonfly = in the air** **fish = under a water lily** **turtle = on the grass** **worm = on the ground** **duck = in the water** **water lily = in the water** **frog = on a water lily** **aquatic plant = under the water** **rock = on the ground**
FOLLOW-UP 📖 *GREEN ENGLISH DICTIONARY EXTENSION*	Make a poster about the pond.

The Pond LEVEL A

Green English
Environmental Education in English

WORKSHEET TITLE	7.2 Let's Make a Mini-pond
SPECIFIC AIMS	<u>Communicative functions</u>: giving and following instructions. <u>Vocabulary</u>: materials and objects (**plastic, bowl, bag, soil, stone, twig, water, plant, stones**). <u>Structures</u>: imperative (**cut, put, make, decorate, take, fill, cover), What's ... in (+ language)?**
MATERIALS NEEDED	Stationery, and for each group of students: a basin or a plastic bowl, a big plastic bag (even a rubbish bag), soil, stones, pebbles, twigs for decoration, water.
PROCEDURE	1. The teacher asks the students to draw the materials in the boxes. **Draw the materials we need in these boxes...** If the students do not know the words, the teacher encourages them to ask the meanings with: **What is soil in (+ language)? And stones?** 2. In groups, the students read and follow the instructions and make a mini-pond. When they don't understand a word, they can ask the teacher using: **What is 'hole' in (+ native language)?** **What is bowl?**
FOLLOW-UP 📖 *GREEN ENGLISH DICTIONARY EXTENSION*	Students can observe the pond after one, two, three and more weeks and record any changes.

WORKSHEET TITLE	**7.3 Pond Record**
SPECIFIC AIMS	<u>Communicative functions:</u> saying dates, describing places. <u>Vocabulary:</u> dates (**numbers, months**), vocabulary related to the pond (**water, frog, dragonfly, fish, duck, water lily, turtle, aquatic plant, worm, ground, ground, rock...**). <u>Structures:</u> **What's the date today? Can / can't. There is... / there isn't.... There are ... / there aren't. Some/any.**
MATERIALS NEEDED	Stationery, magnifying glass, pond or mini-pond.
PROCEDURE	1. This activity should be repeated over a period of time to give students the opportunity to develop observation skills related to a specific environment and see how this environment can change. The teacher brings the students to the pond and students observe it (worksheet 7.2). The teacher asks: **What's the date today?** The students write the date in the box. 2. A visit to the pond: the teacher asks the students to make some simple sentences using the keywords on the worksheet: **Can you see ducks? Ok, then write: it's "I can see ducks..."** **Are there any frogs? Yes, there are some frogs...** 3. Observation of the mini-pond: observation of a sample of water, seaweed, small animals with a magnifying glass **What can you see?** **Are there any...?**
FOLLOW-UP 📖 *GREEN ENGLISH DICTIONARY EXTENSION*	Look on the internet for photos of aquatic plants and make a poster.

Green English
Environmental Education in English

WORKSHEET TITLE	**7.4 Game: Stepping Stones**
SPECIFIC AIMS	Communicative functions: asking questions and answering. Vocabulary: related to the pond (**pond, frog, dragonfly, water, water lily, butterfly, stone, pond, bamboo**), colours, numbers, **elephant, leaf, bee, motorbike, picture**. Structures: Wh-questions, **How many...?**
MATERIALS NEEDED	Stationery, scissors.
PROCEDURE	1. The students cut out the question cards on the second page of the cut-out pages and the frog squares on the first page. **Go to the cut out pages and cut out the cards and the frogs.** 2. The teacher shows students the worksheet and divides them into pairs or groups of three. **This is a game! Look at the numbers...** 3. The teacher plays the game with a student as an example: a player takes a card from the deck and reads the question. **It's my turn to pick a card and read... What's water in your language?** **Do you know? Yes, it's...** If the student answers correctly, he/she goes to the next stone, otherwise he/she stays in place. Whoever gets to the last stone first wins the game. **Then I go to the next stone...** 4. The students play in pairs or in groups of three taking turns asking questions. **It's your turn now.**
FOLLOW-UP 📖 *GREEN ENGLISH DICTIONARY EXTENSION*	Play the game again on "stones" (either in the classroom or gym). Invent new questions and make new question cards.

WORKSHEET TITLE	🎧 **7.5 Five Little Speckled Frogs**
SPECIFIC AIMS	<u>Communicative functions:</u> describing. <u>Vocabulary:</u> numbers, adjectives (**little, speckled, delicious, nice, cool**), nouns (**frog, log, pool**). <u>Structures:</u> adjective order (**five little speckled frogs**).
MATERIALS NEEDED (FACT FILE 12)	FACT FILE about frogs.
PROCEDURE	1. The students observe the pictures of the frogs on the Fact file and describe them out loud. The teacher asks the students some questions. **How many legs has a frog got?** **What can it do? Can it fly? What colour is it?** 2. The teacher plays the song from GREEN ENGLISH CD - TRACK 5). The students listen to it for the first time without reading the words and try to listen for as many words as possible. **Write all the words you understand.** **What is the song about? Is it about dogs?** 3. The students listen to the song again observing the worksheet. **Now listen to the song again and look at the words...** 4. Using the music only (GREEN ENGLISH CD - TRACK 6), the students sing the song and they can either clap their hands or use drums or musical instruments. **Let's sing together...**
FOLLOW-UP 📖 *GREEN ENGLISH DICTIONARY EXTENSION* (FACT FILE 12)	Act out the song: students pretend to be frogs and jump into a fantasy pond. This could be also done in team-teaching with the music teacher.

WORKSHEET TITLE	**8.1 Bug Hunt**
SPECIFIC AIMS	<u>Communicative functions:</u> expressing quantity, identifying animals. ized<u>Vocabulary:</u> bugs (**grasshopper, ladybird, bee, butterfly, caterpillar, dragonfly, beetle, ant, pond-skater**), other small animals (**worm, spider, snail**). <u>Structures:</u> **What can you see...? I can see ...**
MATERIALS NEEDED	Stationery, a park or garden is needed to carry out this activity in order to observe bugs.
PROCEDURE	1. In a garden or park, the students observe the worksheet. While the teacher pronounces the names of the bugs in random order, the students point to them on the worksheet. **Dragonfly. Point to the dragonfly.** **Pond-skater. Show me the picture of the pond-skater.** 2. The teacher then gives some time to the students to look for some bugs: **In English we call them 'bugs.' Now go and find them!** **You have ...10 minutes!** 3. The students look for the bugs and, with the help of the teacher, they check off whether or not they have found them. **Tick or cross. Are there any butterflies?** 4. They complete the sentence at the bottom of the worksheet. 5. Back in the classroom, the students can make a poster of the bugs they found. **Let's make a poster. Draw a spider.**
FOLLOW-UP 📖 *GREEN ENGLISH DICTIONARY EXTENSION* FACT FILES 9-10	The teacher can use FACT FILES Butterflies and Moths and Bug Detective to teach more about the topic.

Green English
Environmental Education in English

A

WORKSHEET TITLE	**8.2 Make Your Bug**
SPECIFIC AIMS	<u>Communicative functions:</u> giving and following instructions. **<u>Vocabulary:</u>** materials (**plastic bottle, glue, cardboard, sticky tape**), parts of the body (**head, body, antennae, legs, eyes, mouth, wings, tail**), animals (**frog, butterfly, ladybird, spider, dragonfly, bee...**). <u>Structures:</u> Imperative.
MATERIALS NEEDED (FACT FILE 13)	FACT FILE **Make a Bug** (with a plastic bottle) Stationery, plastic bottles (one for each student), coloured cardboard (used material brought from home like household packaging), glue, sticky tape. For decoration: buttons, wool, dry legumes, and other reusable materials.
PROCEDURE	1. The students observe the materials on the worksheet. They draw and label the materials brought from home that they can re-use. **What have you got? Wow, buttons... they're so beautiful ... we can re-use them!** 2. The teacher says: **What can we do with all these things?** **We can make a ...** The students try to guess what they are going to do (make a bug). Then, they decide what bug to make with the help of the FACT FILE or can think of one of their own. **What about a ladybird? Or a dragonfly?** 3. The teacher asks the students to draw their bugs in the Project Plan box. **Draw your favourite bug in the 'Project Plan.'** After they have drawn their bugs, they label the parts of the body and the materials needed to make them. **What can you use to make the eyes? Buttons? ... beans?** 4. They make their bugs.
FOLLOW-UP 📖 *GREEN ENGLISH DICTIONARY* *EXTENSION*	Have an exhibit / stand to display their bugs.

WORKSHEET TITLE	🎧 **8.3 A Story: Mr Caterpillar**
SPECIFIC AIMS	<u>Communicative functions</u>: describing pictures and telling stories, describing actions in progress. <u>Vocabulary</u>: vocabulary related to actions (**crawl, eat, work, sleep, snore, become**). <u>Structures</u>: present simple and present continuous.
MATERIALS NEEDED	Stationery.
PROCEDURE	1. The teacher explains to students that they will listen to the story of Mr. Caterpillar. **This is the story of Mr Caterpillar.** 2. The teacher asks the students to find the caterpillar hidden in the drawings: **Look at the picture number 1. Find Mr Caterpillar. Where is he? Is Mr. Caterpillar under a leaf?** 3. The teacher uses students' answers to imitate the caterpillar's actions in the various figures. **Yes, Maria, you're right, Mr Caterpillar is under the leaf... he's crawling, like this...** **What about the second picture? Where is Mr Caterpillar? Is he sleeping? No. He's hungry... He's eating.** Repeat the procedure with the other figures. **Then Mr Caterpillar is tired. Look at this picture... Yes, he's sleeping.** 4. The class listens to the story (GREEN ENGLISH AUDIO CD - TRACK 7) and mimes the caterpillar's story. **Let's mime the actions. ...Mr Caterpillar crawls... Mr Caterpillar eats.**
FOLLOW-UP 📖 *GREEN ENGLISH DICTIONARY EXTENSION* (FACT FILES 7-8)	FACT FILE Insects: Body Parts 2. FACT FILE Silkworms. Make a wormery of silkworms in class.

Green English
Environmental Education in English

A

WORKSHEET TITLE	**8.4 Butterfly Life Cycle**
SPECIFIC AIMS	<u>Communicative functions:</u> telling a sequence of facts. <u>Vocabulary:</u> vocabulary related to butterflies (**egg, cocoon, caterpillar, butterfly, leaf**). <u>Structures:</u> present simple, **Can you see..., Where is ...?,** short answers.
MATERIALS NEEDED	Stationery.
PROCEDURE	1. The students observe the pictures at the top of the worksheet: **This is the life cycle of a butterfly. From a tiny egg to a fat caterpillar and then to a beautiful butterfly...** 2. The teacher asks the students to identify the pictures in the six boxes. **Look at the pictures. Where can you see the cocoon?** 3. The students re-order the story of the butterfly from 1 to 6 with the help of the pictures at the top of the worksheet. **Write the numbers in the boxes to re-order the story of the caterpillar...** **KEY:** **1. On a leaf in the garden there is a tiny egg.** **2. The egg goes "POP!!!" Out comes a tiny caterpillar.** **3. The caterpillar eats some leaves.** **4. The caterpillar goes to sleep in a cocoon.** **5. The caterpillar wakes up and...** **6. ...it 's a beautiful butterfly!!!** 4. The teacher asks the students to take turns and read the sentences, or the teacher reads the sentences out loud and the students must identify them on the worksheet. The students colour the black and white pictures.
FOLLOW-UP 📖 *GREEN ENGLISH DICTIONARY* *EXTENSION* (FACT FILES 8 -9)	The teacher can keep some silkworms in class and have the students observe them (use the FACT FILE Silkworms); have students carry out a research project on the various species of butterflies in the area (in collaboration with an environmental education centre or with the science teacher). The FACT FILE Butterflies and Moths can be used to make a poster.

WORKSHEET TITLE	**8.5 How to Make a Wormery**
SPECIFIC AIMS	Communicative functions: giving and following instructions. Vocabulary: materials, objects (**jar, plastic bottle, soil, sand, sticky tape, elastic band, leaves, grass, food, mesh, lid, paper**). Structures: imperative (**cut, put, add, wrap, fix, cover, leave, take off, draw, see**).
MATERIALS NEEDED	Stationery, for groups of 4 students: a big and wide glass jar, a plastic bottle, damp soil, sand (not beach sand), sticky tape, an elastic band, leaves and grass, mesh, black paper, worms (kept hidden till the very last moment to surprise the students. They can be found in a compost - where they are fat and happy - or in a fishing shop).
PROCEDURE	1. The teacher asks students to guess what "wormery" means. **What is a wormery? Can you guess?** The teacher doesn't tell them if they are right or not by saying: **Surprise, surprise! You will soon find out!!!** 2. The students draw the materials in the boxes. **Draw the materials in the boxes.** 3. In groups of 4, they follow the instructions on the second half of the worksheet until number 4. The teacher goes from group to group helping them. **Cut the plastic bottle like this... Good... Then you put it in the jar...** 4. After everyone has done the first 4 sentences, the teacher takes out the jar/bag of worms creating an atmosphere of suspense and passes them out to the students who then put them in the jars. **I've got long, thin, slimy worms and short, fat, juicy worms. They are our new pets! Aren't they lovely?** 5. The students do sentences 6 and 7. **Let's put the worms in the their new home... So what's a wormery? Yes, it's a home for worms!** 6. After a couple of days the students can take off the black paper from the wormeries and observe what they see (they should see the tunnels that the worms made). **What can you see? Can you see the tunnels? Yes? Draw what you see. Let's set them free, because we respect all creatures!** (the teacher can also use the Green English Keywords in *worksheet* 1.3). After some time, the worms are set free either in a garden or kitchen garden having perhaps a "good-bye party."
FOLLOW-UP 📖 *GREEN ENGLISH DICTIONARY* *EXTENSION*	Listen to the song: **I think I'll go eat worms** on the website **http://www.niehs.nih.gov/kids/lyrics/worms.htm**

TITOLO SCHEDA	**9.1 See, Smell, Touch**
SPECIFIC AIMS	<u>Communicative functions:</u> expressing sensory perceptions. <u>Vocabulary:</u> natural elements and other elements, vocabulary related to senses (**see, smell, touch, hear, feel**). <u>Structures:</u> **can you ..., what can you ...?**
MATERIALS NEEDED	Stationery, an area outside (garden).
PROCEDURE	1. The teacher takes the students outside and asks them to observe, listen, touch and smell the surrounding natural and non-natural elements. The students draw or write in the correct boxes. **Look around... What can you see? Draw / write in the correct box. You see with your ... (elicit 'eyes')...** 2. Repeat the same thing with the other senses. **Listen, touch, smell.** **Give some examples.** **Yuck! That's disgusting! Mmmm, delicious... Lovely! Wonderful! Beautiful!** 3. The students complete the sentences and compare what they see, feel and smell. **Lucia, what can you hear? The cars... Oh, sure... Can you hear the train...?**
FOLLOW-UP 📖 *GREEN ENGLISH DICTIONARY EXTENSION*	Survey: ask students what their favourite sense is (see, smell, touch, hear).

See, Smell, Touch LEVEL A

Green English
Environmental Education in English

WORKSHEET TITLE	9.2 A Feely-box
SPECIFIC AIMS	<u>Communicative functions</u>: identifying objects. <u>Vocabulary</u>: objects (**shoe box, scissors**), various objects (**button, apple, cotton, twig, spider, leaf, banana, flower, pencil, carrot, paper clip ...**). <u>Structures</u>: imperative (**put, ask**), **What is it? It's ...**
MATERIALS NEEDED	Stationery, 1 shoe box for every 4-5 students, various objects to show students (ex: buttons, leaf, cotton, twig, vegetables, fruit, plastic animals, etc ...), scissors.
PROCEDURE	1. The students are divided into teams of 4-5. They draw the objects they brought to class in the given box, labelling them. **Draw your objects in the box. Label them.** 2. In their teams, the students prepare the feely box. **Make a hole on one side of your box.** They put some objects in the box and the groups swap boxes. **Put some objects in the box.** **Now give, the box to another team.** 3. The students take turns putting a hand in the hole and guessing what's inside the box. **Take it in turns, put your hand in the box.** **Guess what's in the box.** 4. The students write down the objects they touched, putting the objects they guessed and didn't guess into the right column. **What did you guess? Write the list here.**
FOLLOW-UP 📖 *GREEN ENGLISH DICTIONARY EXTENSION*	Make a 'touch picture' collage for their journals using various kinds of materials that are different to the touch (smooth, bumpy, soft...).

Green English
Environmental Education in English

A

WORKSHEET TITLE	9.3 Let's Make a Herb Potpourri
SPECIFIC AIMS	<u>Communicative functions:</u> identifying and describing objects, following instructions, expressing quantity. <u>Vocabulary:</u> aromatic herbs (**herb, basil, parsley, mint, lavender, sage, oregano, rosemary, camomile, cloves, thyme**), adjectives (**lovely, yucky, nice**), numbers, objects (**cup, cloth, ribbon**). <u>Structures:</u> **What is it? What is it like?**
MATERIALS NEEDED	Stationery, blindfold, aromatic plants (fresh and dried if possible): parsley, sage, rosemary, thyme, mint, basil, oregano, camomile, lavender, sweet marjoram, cloves, scissors, a square of cloth and a ribbon for each student.
PROCEDURE	1. The students smell the different aromatic herbs. **Smell the herbs!** They draw a smiley face on the herbs they like. **What is it like? Is it yucky?** 2. The students have to identify the fresh and dried herbs while blindfolded: **What is it? Yes, it's camomile.** 3. The teacher explains what potpourri is and what it is used for. **A potpourri mixture is a mixture of dried herbs. It smells nice. You can put it in your wardrobe.** 4. The students have to identify the herbs in the photographs looking at the dried herbs. **Look at the photographs. Can you see mint?** They then write the names of the herbs under the photos. **Write the names of the herbs.** 5. The students cut the herbs and put them in the cloth, closing it with the ribbon. **Cut the herbs and put them in the cloth.** **Tie the cloth with the ribbon.**
FOLLOW-UP 📖 *GREEN ENGLISH DICTIONARY EXTENSION*	Listen to the song **Scarborough Fair** by Simon & Garfunkel **www.contemplator.com/tunebook/england/scarboro.htm** Herb classification record / poster: dry some herbs in class, paste them on a piece of paper/cardboard and label them. Research on the medicinal properties of herbs. Survey: Which herbs do you use at home?

The House in the Country LEVEL A

Green English
Environmental Education in English

WORKSHEET TITLE	**10.1 The Farmhouse**
SPECIFIC AIMS	<u>Communicative functions:</u> describing rooms. <u>Vocabulary:</u> rooms in the house (**kitchen, shed, bedroom, fireplace, stable, well, bathroom, chimney, stove, table, chair...**), farm animals (**chicken, cock, chicks, pig, cow, horse, donkey, duck**). <u>Structures:</u> **What is there...? Where is the ...? There is / There are ..., How many...?**
MATERIALS NEEDED	Stationery, scissors, glue.
PROCEDURE	1. The students go to the cut out page, cut out the pictures and paste the missing ones in the right place. **Go to the cut out page. Cut the pictures and paste them in the right place.** 2. When the students have finished pasting the pictures, they cover the page and take turns asking each other questions. They can answer either out loud or by pointing. **What is there in the kitchen?** **What is there in the bedroom?** **Where is the duck?** **Where is the well?** **How many chicks are there?** **...**
FOLLOW-UP 📖 *GREEN ENGLISH DICTIONARY EXTENSION*	Make a farm using recycled or natural materials: shoe box, wood, coloured pieces of wool or fabric etc ...) A school trip to a farm.

Green English
Environmental Education in English

A

WORKSHEET TITLE	**10.2 Farm Animals**
SPECIFIC AIMS	<u>Communicative functions:</u> talking about what animals do. <u>Vocabulary:</u> farm animals (**chicken, cow, pig, sheep, chicks, cock, donkey, horse**), animal calls (**oink-oink, moo, cluck-cluck, cock-a-doodle-doo, neigh, cheep-cheep, baa, hee-haw**). <u>Structures:</u> **What...?** present simple (**produce, do, wake up, come from, work, smell**).
MATERIALS NEEDED	Stationery.
PROCEDURE	1. The students draw arrows to match the animals to their functions. **Match the animals to their function. What do they produce? What do they do?** The teacher asks the students some questions. **Which animals produce milk? Which animals work?** 2. The students cut out the animal calls from the cut out pages and they paste them in the given bubbles: **What does the pig say? And the sheep?** **KEY:** **COCK-A-DOODLE-DOO cock - They wake us up** **NEIGH horse - They run fast** **CHEEP-CHEEP chicks - They come from eggs** **BAA sheep - They produce wool** **MOO cow - They produce milk** **OINK-OINK pig - They smell** **CLUCK-CLUCK hen - They produce eggs** **HEE-HAW donkey - They work hard**
FOLLOW-UP 📖 *GREEN ENGLISH DICTIONARY EXTENSION*	Make a poster of a **Crazy Farm** where wild animals are raised (lion...) or where the animals produce imaginative products (hens laying golden eggs, chocolate milk...) Listen to the song: **Old McDonald...** http://www.kididdles.com/mouseum/o009.html

WORKSHEET TITLE	**10.3 Save Energy in Your House**
SPECIFIC AIMS	<u>Communicative functions:</u> comparing and describing habits. <u>Vocabulary:</u> rooms and objects in the house (**bathroom, sitting room, bedroom, kitchen, stairs, light, window, tap, bin, heating, room**), adjectives (**on, off, open, closed**), **rubbish, brush, teeth**. <u>Structures:</u> **There is ... / There are ...**, the verb **to be**, prepositions.
MATERIALS NEEDED	Stationery.
PROCEDURE	1. The students look at the two pictures and find the four differences. **Spot the differences in the two pictures. What can you see? In the first picture the lights are...?** **KEY:** **bathroom: tap on / tap off** **sitting room: window open / window closed** **bedroom: light on / light off** **kitchen: waste water / save water, no recycling / recycling** 2. The teacher helps the students understand the sentences. The students then choose the right habit. **Look at these sentences...** **What is correct when you brush your teeth?** **And when the heating is on, do you keep windows open or closed?** **KEY:** **tap off - windows closed - lights off - different bins.**
FOLLOW-UP 📖 *GREEN ENGLISH DICTIONARY EXTENSION* (FACT FILE 1)	FACT FILE Help the Environment.

Green English
Environmental Education in English

A

WORKSHEET TITLE	**10.4 A Mobile for your Room**
SPECIFIC AIMS	<u>Communicative functions</u>: talking about your favourite... <u>Vocabulary</u>: materials (**twigs, string, cardboard, felt pen, sticky tape, scissors, glue**), natural elements (**flower, leaf, fruit, bug**), vocabulary based on students' answers. <u>Structures</u>: **My favourite ... is...**
MATERIALS NEEDED	Stationery, twigs, string, cardboard even if used, felt pens, scissors, glue, sticky tape, used coloured paper (gift wrapping paper, tin foil...), Fact Files or nature/gardening magazines.
PROCEDURE	1. The students look through the FACT FILES or magazines for their favourite flower, leaf, fruit or bug. **Look at the pictures and choose your favourite things.** 2. The students write down what they have chosen and draw it on the worksheet. **Draw your favourite flower / fruit / leaf / bug on the worksheet.** 3. They then draw and colour the same elements again on cardboard, but bigger, with more details and using various materials. **Make a flower / a leaf / a fruit / a bug.** **Draw and decorate your favourite things.** 4. They cut out their drawings and make their mobiles by observing the pictures and following the instructions. **Stick a piece of string on the flower. Use sticky tape. Make a cross with the twigs. Fix the twigs with tape. Tie the strings on the twigs. Do you like it? Hang your mobile in your room.**
FOLLOW-UP 🎧 AUDIO CD Track 64 📖 *GREEN ENGLISH DICTIONARY EXTENSION*	Listen to the song **'My Favourite Things'** by Rodgers-Hammerstein Raindrops on roses and whiskers on kittens Bright copper kettles and warm woollen mittens Brown paper packages tied up with strings These are a few of my favourite things Cream coloured ponies and crisp apple streudels Doorbells and sleigh bells and schnitzel with noodles Wild geese that fly with the moon on their wings These are a few of my favourite things Girls in white dresses with blue satin sashes Snowflakes that stay on my nose and eyelashes Silver white winters that melt into springs These are a few of my favourite things When the dog bites When the bee stings When I'm feeling sad I simply remember my favourite things And then I don't feel so bad.

WORKSHEET TITLE	🎧 **1.1 A Green English Project**
SPECIFIC AIMS	<u>Communicative functions:</u> following instructions, talking about environmentally-friendly habits, giving and asking for personal information. <u>Vocabulary:</u> vocabulary related to the environment (**nature, environment, paper, air, energy, water**). <u>Structures:</u> present simple, imperative (**respect, save, recycle, reduce, re-use, don't pollute**).
MATERIALS NEEDED	Stationery, glue, a photo of each student, a ring binder with A4 plastic pockets for each student.
PROCEDURE	1. The teacher asks the students to paste their photos in the given space and then asks them to fill in **"My green ID."** **Fill in your Green ID.** The students read the sentences in the box and underline the keywords. 2. The teacher encourages the students to participate: **Let's read the worksheet!** **I love nature. I love animals, plants, trees, flowers.** **Do you love nature?** **Respect nature. Respect plants ... Animals, plants are all living creatures...** **Respect the environment: what is the environment?** **It's the world around us.** **Oh look! Here's a piece of paper. Paper is precious.** **Save paper: use both sides ... this side and that side.** **Recycle, reduce and reuse plastic bottles, cans and paper.** **Do you recycle?** **Don't pollute water and air. Pollution makes air and water dirty. Help keep the air clean: ride a bike or walk to school.** **Do you come to school by bike?** **Save energy: water, electricity ...** 3. The teacher asks the students to choose their favourite motto and to write it in the bubble. **What's your favourite motto? Is it "I love nature"? Write your favourite sentence.** 4. The teacher asks the students to colour and decorate the cover and paste it onto the Journal (an A4 ring binder with plastic pockets) and explains that it will grow along with them as they put their work into it.
FOLLOW-UP	Students prepare the **Green English Dictionary**. The teacher photocopies the letters of the alphabet on page 130 of this guide and gives them to the students. They cut out the letters, paste them into a notebook and colour them in. Students should allow 3-4 pages for each letter so that they can write down and illustrate the new words.

Green English
Environmental Education in English

B

WORKSHEET TITLE	**1.2 Green English Commandments**
SPECIFIC AIMS	Communicative functions: talking about environmentally-friendly habits. Vocabulary: words related to positive values and behaviour (**helpful, friend, smart, precious**) and to the environment (**plants, animals, nature, chemicals, pesticides, non-organic waste, everything, everybody, toys, intrusions, rubbish, water, electricity**). Structures: imperative (**respect, do not destroy, don't litter, be, reduce, reuse, recycle, don't waste**).
MATERIALS NEEDED	Stationery, felt tip pens, a sheet of paper.

PROCEDURE	1. The teacher reads the commandments and students listen. **Listen carefully.**
	
	    1 - Respect! Plants and animals are not toys! Do not destroy them.
	    2 - Nature doesn't like chemicals, pesticides and non-organic waste. Don't litter!
	    3 - Be smart and helpful! Be a good friend for everything and everybody.
	    4 - Rubbish is precious! Reduce, reuse, or recycle it.
	    5 - Water and electricity are precious! Don't waste them.
	
	2. The students cut out the commandments and paste them in the right order on another sheet of paper.
	Cut and paste the five commandments in the correct order.
	
	3. The class reads each sentence while the teacher encourages students to think about the meaning.
	Now let's read the sentences...
	Do you use rechargeable batteries?
	How can we save water?

FOLLOW-UP 📖 *GREEN ENGLISH DICTIONARY EXTENSION*	A miming game: a student mimes the actions of a commandment and the other students have to guess which one it is. Students can write a report of the "bad" habits they have observed while at home or outside. Students can draw pictures with captions underneath: my brother wastes water! This can be added to the journal.

B

The Orchard LEVEL B

WORSHEET TITLE	**2.1 My tree**
SPECIFIC AIMS	<u>Communicative functions:</u> describing the characteristics and sizes of trees in detail, expressing age, formulating a hypothesis, dividing. <u>Vocabulary:</u> sizes (**big, medium, small**), measurements (**centimetres**), numbers above 100 and with decimals (**two point five**), characteristics (**colour, girth, height, smell, nice, yuck**). <u>Structures:</u> **It is … It has got …, How old …? It's … high/years old**, imperative (**choose, observe, smell, guess, measure, divide**).
MATERIALS NEEDED	Stationery, measuring tape.
PROCEDURE	1. The teacher brings the students to the school garden or in a public garden and asks them to choose a tree. **Choose a tree!** 2. The teacher gathers the students with a signal (a whistle, a bell …) and explains the first task. The students then go back to their trees to carry out the procedure. This procedure is carried out for each task: - the size of the tree **Observe the size of your tree. Is it big?…** - smell **Now use your nose and smell your tree.** **Mmm, it's nice!! / Yuck, it's horrible!** - colour **Observe the colour of the leaves** **Write the colour(s) on your worksheet.** 3. The teacher explains to the students that they are going to try to calculate how old the tree is and how tall it is. For a tree's age, the girth is measured at a height of 1.5 metres from the ground and then this is divided by 2.5 cm, since a tree grows approximately 2.5 cm a year. **How old is your tree?** **First measure the girth of your tree.** **Now divide this by 2.5 cm.** **80 cm divided by 2.5 is 32.** **This is 32 years old. How old is your tree?** 4. As for the height of the tree, the students try to guess it by imagining how many people it takes, one on top of the other, to reach the height of the tree. **Guess the height of your tree.** In pairs, the students measure the height of the tree with a pencil. The teacher explains the activity using FACT FILE **How to measure a tree.**
FOLLOW-UP	Analyse the characteristics of leaves (lobed, toothed, etc.) using FACT FILE **Leaf Classification** and of trees using FACT FILE **Types of Trees**. Make a 'Tree Classification' poster describing the characteristics of different trees.

(FACT FILE 4)

📖 *GREEN ENGLISH DICTIONARY EXTENSION*

(FACT FILES 16 -3)

WORKSHEET TITLE	2.2 How Old Are You?
SPECIFIC AIMS	<u>Communicative functions:</u> asking about and saying ages (present and past) and years of birth. <u>Vocabulary:</u> numbers 0-100, natural elements (**tree stump, ring**). <u>Structures:</u> **How old are you? How old is the tree? I'm ... It's ... When were you born? In 1999, When was it born?, Was/were.**
MATERIALS NEEDED	Stationery, a tree stump to see the rings (or a photo).
PROCEDURE	1. The teacher shows the students the tree stump and tells them, for example, that a young tree was born in 1990. **This tree was born in ... (nineteen-ninety).** 2. The teacher asks the students to draw a small circle in the middle of the page. **Draw a small ring in the middle of the page. The teacher asks the students to write the year inside the circle. Write 1990 inside the ring.** 3. The teacher explains that each year the tree produces a new ring. **Each year the tree forms a new ring.** The students add other rings around the first one until they reach the present year and they write the years inside each ring. **Write 1991 inside this ring.** 4. The teacher asks each student to colour in the ring in which they were born. Ask each student one at a time so they can all have turns answering. **How old are you? When were you born? In ... Colour the ring.**
FOLLOW-UP 📖 *GREEN ENGLISH DICTIONARY EXTENSION*	A quiz game. The students can answer questions in teams. Examples of questions: How old was the tree in 1994? How old were you in 1999? etc.

The Orchard LEVEL B

Green English
Environmental Education in English

WORKSHEET TITLE	**2.3 How to Read a Tree Stump**
SPECIFIC AIMS	<u>Communicative functions:</u> describing facts. <u>Vocabulary:</u> adjectives related to quality (**light, soft, dark, hard, hot, wide, narrow**), seasons (**summer, spring**), natural elements (**tree, tree stump, rings, layer, leaves, roots, water, rain**), objects (**magnifying glass, wall**). <u>Structures:</u> present simple (**grows, stops, cut, doesn't have**).
MATERIALS NEEDED	Tree stump or picture of one, magnifying glass.
PROCEDURE	1. The teacher tells the students that the rings of the tree stump can be different. **Each ring is made of a light, soft layer and a dark, hard layer.** **Look at this layer. Is it light or dark? Is it soft or hard?** **This layer grows in spring. Yes, the light, soft layer grows in spring.** **And this layer is... Yes, it's dark and hard. It grows in summer.** **Look at the rings on this tree stump. Some are narrow, like this one. Look, this one is wide ... yes! Very wide!** 2. The teacher explains the four situations in order using gestures and pictures. **Look at picture number 1 - The tree grows and grows ... yes, very rapidly.** The teacher then asks the students to guess what kind of rings the tree produces in each one. **What are these rings like? Are they narrow or wide?** 3. The students observe the pictures and put a number corresponding to the description into the boxes. **KEY:** **3 = barrow rings and wide rings** **1 = wide rings** **2 = narrow rings on one side** **4 = narrow rings**
FOLLOW-UP 📖 *GREEN ENGLISH DICTIONARY EXTENSION*	Storytelling: with the help of the teacher, students can make up a story about the life of their favourite tree and act it out. Worksheets 2.1 and 2.2 can be tied up to this activity.

WORKSHEET TITLE	**2.4 Fruit Calendar**
SPECIFIC AIMS	<u>Communicative functions:</u> asking information about facts, expressing preferences. <u>Vocabulary:</u> fruit (**almond, apple, apricot, blackberry, blueberry, cherry, chestnut, fig, grapefruit, grapes, hazelnut, kiwi, lemon, melon, orange, peach, pear, persimmon, plum, raspberry, strawberry, tangerine, walnut, watermelon**), months (**January, February, March, … December**), seasons (**Spring, Summer, Autumn, Winter**). <u>Structures:</u> present simple, **When do … ripen? What's your favourite fruit? Do you like…?**
MATERIALS NEEDED (FACT FILE 18)	Stationery, FACT FILE **Fruit Calendar** (or information about the ripening seasons of fruits in a given country or area of the world), pictures of fruit.
PROCEDURE	1. The teacher introduces the names of the fruit using pictures and encourages them to answer some questions: **This is a cherry. Do you like cherries?** **What colour are they?** 2. The teacher asks the students to guess when the different fruits ripen. **When do cherries ripen?** **When are there cherries in the orchard?** 3. The students draw the fruits that are ripe in each of the months. **Draw a cherry in June.** 4. The teacher asks the students to complete the sentence at the bottom of the worksheet with **My favourite fruit grows in …**
FOLLOW-UP 📖 *GREEN ENGLISH DICTIONARY EXTENSION*	Divide the months into groups according to the seasons they fall under. Invent riddles about fruit. For example: **It's the name of a colour. What is it?** **They ripen in May and June. What are they?** Add other fruits or locally found fruits to the calendar or create a similar one.

WORKSHEET TITLE	**2.5 How to Make Jam** Note: If it's not possible to make jam for logistic reasons, the students can mime and draw the actions.
SPECIFIC AIMS	<u>Communicative functions</u>: following and giving instructions. <u>Vocabulary</u>: ingredients (**fruit, sugar, water**), quantities (**3 cups, 1 cup**), cooking vocabulary (**pot, gas stove, jar, bread, butter, jam**), time expressions (**minutes**). <u>Structures</u>: imperative (**peel, wash, stone, chop, put, boil, remove, wait, eat**).
MATERIALS NEEDED	Fruit (example: peaches + one banana that works as a natural pectin to thicken the jam). All fruit is peeled and stoned for this activity. The procedure can be changed according to the fruit that is being used. Sugar, water, knives, pot, ladle, jars, a heating source (gas stove) and stationery.
PROCEDURE	1. The teacher uses gestures and draws pictures to help explain the various steps to making jam. **First we peel the fruit (if it's necessary).** The teacher repeats the explanation (**wash, peel, stone, chop, add water and sugar, boil...**) for each step. 2. The students draw the missing instructions in the empty spaces. 3. The students follow the instructions and make the jam. The teacher helps especially during the difficult steps (chopping, boiling...) **Let's make our jam.**
FOLLOW-UP 📖 *GREEN ENGLISH DICTIONARY EXTENSION*	Use the song **This is the way ...** to sing the instructions (using the traditional tune). **This is the way we wash the fruit** **wash the fruit, wash the fruit** **To make our jam** **This is the way ... we peel the fruit** **We chop the fruit / - We put it in a pot** **We boil the fruit / - We add the sugar** **We wait 2 minutes / - We put into jars** **We eat it up!** The jars of jam can be used as gifts to give to parents or friends.

WORKSHEET TITLE	🎧 **3.1 A True Story: The Plant Cycle**
SPECIFIC AIMS	<u>Communicative functions</u>: describing the phases of a natural process. <u>Vocabulary</u>: vocabulary related to nature (**seed, roots, seedling, leaves, flower, ground, sun, rain**), time expressions (**after some time, then**). <u>Structures</u>: present simple (**grow, appear, water, warm, fall**).
MATERIALS NEEDED	Stationery, a small plant in a vase (such as sunflowers or daisies), seeds, seedlings or some pictures of the various parts of a plant.
PROCEDURE	1. The teacher introduces the vocabulary at the top of the worksheet using the pictures to help explain their meanings. **Look! This is a seed...** 2. The teacher reads the sentences in order or plays the CD (GREEN ENGLISH AUDIO CD - TRACK 18). **KEY:** **The seed is asleep under the ground.** **Then the rain waters the seed.** **The sun warms it.** **Roots grow.** **The seedling grows and grows.** **After some time leaves appear.** **A flower grows on the plant.** **Then seeds fall from the flower.** 3. The students have to fill in the blanks. **Listen and fill in the blanks:** **The seed is asleep under the ground. What word is missing?** **Yes, seed. Write seed.** **The seed is asleep. Good night seed!** **...**
FOLLOW-UP 📖 *GREEN ENGLISH DICTIONARY EXTENSION*	Planting a seed in the classroom or outside. See worksheet 6.1.

WORKSHEET TITLE	**3.2 Parts of a Plant**
SPECIFIC AIMS	<u>Communicative functions:</u> describing the functions of the various parts of a plant. <u>Vocabulary:</u> parts of a plant (**fruit, flower, seed, roots, stem, leaf**), what plants need (**food, energy, sun, air, water, minerals**), **plant, insects.** <u>Structures:</u> present simple (**produce, take in, carry, anchor, absorb, generate, attract**). **What is it?**
MATERIALS NEEDED	Stationery, a (strawberry) plant with flowers, seeds, fruit, roots, leaves and a stem (or pictures). For follow-up: a celery stalk, coloured ink, a glass jar, water.
PROCEDURE	1. The teacher shows the parts of the plant to the students using the plant or pictures. **These are the parts of a plant: fruit, flower, seeds, roots, leaf and stem.** 2. The students listen to the teacher's instructions and draw in the box. The teacher explains the functions of the various parts of a plant with gestures or by drawing pictures on the board. **Draw a long stem and some leaves. The stem carries water and minerals to the leaves.** Draw water and minerals going through the stem. **Now draw the roots. Roots anchor the plant to the ground and absorb water and minerals.** Draw the roots. **The leaves produce food for the plant. They take in energy from the sun and produce sugar.** Draw the sun. Draw the leaves. Draw arrows pointing to the leaves. **Draw a flower. Flowers attract insects. Draw an insect on the flower.** Draw a strawberry. **Now draw a fruit. The fruit is a seed container.** Draw the seeds. **Draw seeds in the fruit. Seeds generate new plants.** 3. The teacher reads the functions 1-6 and makes sure that students remember the functions of the different parts of a plant. **They take in energy from the sun. What is it? Leaves! Correct!** The students do the matching exercise. **Now write the letters in the correct boxes.** **KEY** **1E – 2F – 3D – 4A – 5C – 6B**
FOLLOW-UP 📖 *GREEN ENGLISH DICTIONARY EXTENSION* (FACT FILE 2)	Use FACT FILE **Parts of a flower.** <u>Experiment.</u> Dip a celery stem in a glass of water mixed with coloured ink and leave it there for a few hours. Once the celery has absorbed the ink-water solution, it is possible to see how the lymph runs through the celery stem.

WORKSHEET TITLE	**3.3 Photosynthesis**
SPECIFIC AIMS	<u>Communicative functions:</u> describing a scientific process. <u>Vocabulary:</u> scientific vocabulary (**process, photosynthesis, energy, sun, water, minerals, carbon dioxide, chlorophyll, sunlight, air, oxygen, sugar, glucose, food, living creatures**). <u>Structures:</u> present simple (**take, trap, absorb, produce, take in, transform, release**).
MATERIALS NEEDED	For the experiment: a plant (one plant for every 2-3 students), a paper clip (for each plant), aluminium foil (for each plant).
PROCEDURE	1. The teacher uses the illustrations and the plants to guide the students in the reading and comprehension of the photosynthesis process. **What can you see here? A plant, and here? The sun.** 2. The teacher illustrates the photosynthesis process placing special attention on some of the scientific terms: **Sun is very important for plants. Why?** **Read here and tell me, what do plants take from the sun? Energy, yes.** The teacher asks questions like: **What do leaves produce? What is carbon dioxide in your language? What is the process called?** 3. The students answer with True or False and correct the false statements using the blanks on the right. **Write T or F for True or False, and then write the correct answer here. KEY:** **1-T, 2-F, 3-T, 4-F, 5-T.** 4. The students do the experiment keeping the leaf on the plant. **Now let's do this experiment: fix a piece of aluminium on a leaf using a paperclip. Leave the plants in the sun.** **We must wait four days and see what happens.** The part of the leaf that is covered with aluminium will be "discoloured". It won't be green like the rest of the leaf because it was deprived of sun-light. The photosynthesis process did not occur in that part of the leaf and therefore lacks chlorophyll. 5. The students take off the aluminium and observe what happened. **What can you see? Draw.**
FOLLOW-UP 📖 *GREEN ENGLISH DICTIONARY EXTENSION*	Observations of a plant kept in the sun and of a plant kept in the dark.

WORKSHEET TITLE	**3.4 Are You a Good Plant-sitter?**
SPECIFIC AIMS	<u>Communicative functions</u>: describing the needs of a plant. <u>Vocabulary</u>: vocabulary related to the house (**freezer, bed, window**), places (**garage, garden, train station**), food (**water, milk, lemonade, drink, hamburgers, pizza**), substances (**gas, smoke, oxygen, compost**), colours (**yellow, green, pink**), prepositions of place (**in, at, under, next to, on**). <u>Structures</u>: Wh- questions (**where, what**), present simple (**keep, eat, live, need**).
MATERIALS NEEDED	Stationery, a prize (a crown made with leaves, a plant, a flower...).
PROCEDURE	1. The teacher divides the students into teams and asks them to choose a name for their teams and a leader: **Choose a name for your team. Choose a leader.** 2. The teacher reads the questions and the teams have to answer. **Choose the right answer.** **KEY:** **near a window - water - compost - green - oxygen - in the garden.** 3. The teacher asks the students to complete the sentences at the bottom of the page. **Now complete the sentences.** 4. The first team to finish all the sentences hands on the worksheet. The team with the most correct answers wins the prize. **The winner is...**
FOLLOW-UP 📖 *GREEN ENGLISH DICTIONARY EXTENSION*	Create other quizzes.

Green English
Environmental Education in English

B

WORKSHEET TITLE	**4.1 What Do You Recycle?**
SPECIFIC AIMS	<u>Communicative functions:</u> talking about past actions, expressing quantity. <u>Vocabulary:</u> days of the week (**Monday, Tuesday, Wednesday, Thursday, Friday, Saturday, Sunday**), recyclable materials (**plastic, glass, paper, organic waste**), quantity (**some, a lot of, too much, no ...**). <u>Structures:</u> On + day of the week, past simple (**there was / were**).
MATERIALS NEEDED	Stationery.
PROCEDURE	1. The teacher explains to the students that they must keep a record of what they throw away for a week. **Keep a daily record of what you throw away. Yes, the rubbish you produce each day: on Monday, on Tuesday ...** 2. After a week the teacher asks: **What was there in your rubbish bin on Monday?** **On Monday there was / were 3 plastic bottles and a lot of paper ...** 3. The students choose the answer to the last question. **Maria, how much rubbish was in your bin last week?** **A lot of rubbish? Too much rubbish? And you Mario?**
FOLLOW-UP 📖 *GREEN ENGLISH DICTIONARY EXTENSION*	Make a poster about rubbish (collage, photos, newspapers...).

WORKSHEET TITLE	**4.2 Make Your Own Compost**
SPECIFIC AIMS	<u>Communicative functions:</u> following instructions, formulating hypotheses. <u>Vocabulary:</u> food (organic material that can be used in a compost such as **banana skin, grass cuttings, dry leaves, leftovers...**), materials and objects (**bottle, organic waste, compost bin**), **top, bottom**, places (**garden**). <u>Structures:</u> imperative (**cut off, put, observe**), present simple question form (**What happens ...? It turns into ...**).
MATERIALS NEEDED	Stationery, transparent plastic bottles (one for each student), organic waste. Note: the bottles need to be cut at either end to form an open-ended cylinder. If the teacher thinks this is too dangerous for the students to do, the teacher can get the bottles ready before the lesson.
PROCEDURE	1. The teacher shows the students the organic waste (potato peel, apple core, lettuce leaf ...) and asks the students: **What is this? Is it plastic? Is it paper?** **No, it isn't. It's organic waste.** **Where do we put it? Yes, we put it in the compost-bins.** 2. The teacher explains that the students can use the plastic bottles to make mini compost-bins. **We can use these bottles to make mini compost-bins.** 3. The teacher asks: **What happens to the organic waste?** **Does it turn into water? Does it turn into plastic?** **Does it turn into compost to feed your plants?** 4. The students follow the procedure to make the mini compost-bins. They then place them in the garden and put small pieces of organic waste into them (fruit peel from break time or other organic waste brought from home). 5. They observe it over time and fill in the chart: **What happens to the organic waste?** **It's smelly... There are insects... It turns into COMPOST.**
FOLLOW-UP 📖 *GREEN ENGLISH DICTIONARY EXTENSION*	Odd-one-out. The students create a chart with various organic materials and one non-organic object (ex. pen, plastic bag, can). They exchange their charts and they have to find the odd-one-out.

WORKSHEET TITLE	**4.3 The Life Cycle of...**
SPECIFIC AIMS	<u>Communicative functions:</u> describing changes and processes. <u>Vocabulary:</u> materials (**plastic, paper, aluminium, glass, sand, wood, oil, bauxite**), terms related to materials (**raw materials, factories, goods, use, rubbish, recycling**). <u>Structures:</u> present simple (**make, become, buy, use, recycle, save**), Wh- questions (**What...? Where...?**)
MATERIALS NEEDED	Stationery, pictures of shops and factories, pictures of raw materials (sand, wood, petrol and bauxite), plastic bottle, glass jar, newspaper, can.
PROCEDURE	1. The teachers shows the raw materials: sand, wood, petrol and bauxite (aluminium). **Sand, wood, oil, and bauxite are raw materials. With sand, wood, oil and bauxite we make plastic, aluminium, glass and paper.** 2. The teacher shows the students the various objects and tells them what they are made of. **This bottle is made of plastic. It's a plastic bottle. And this jar? It's made of glass. The newspaper? It's made of paper. The can is made of aluminium.** 3. The teacher asks the students to match the raw materials to the products: **What is the raw material for glass? The raw material for glass is sand. What is the raw material for paper? It's wood** (Plastic/oil; Aluminium/bauxite). 4. The teacher shows them the picture of the factory: **Where does sand become glass? In a factory.** Show the end products (bottle, jar, etc.). **Then paper, plastic, glass and aluminium become bottles of water, jars of yogurt, cans of coke and newspapers. Where? In other factories.** 5. The teacher shows the pictures of the shops: **Then we buy the bottle of water, the jar of yogurt, the can of coke and the newspaper. These are the goods. Where do we buy goods? In shops.** 6. The teachers mimes the actions using the plastic bottle, the glass jar, the newspaper, and the can. **Then we use the goods. The bottle of water, the jar of yogurt, the can of beer and the newspaper. We drink the water in the bottle, we read the newspaper... and when we have finished, what do we do? We put the jar, the newspaper, the plastic bottle, the can in the rubbish bin. But if we separate our rubbish we can recycle it and save precious raw materials.** 7. The teacher divides the students into groups and asks each group to choose a recyclable material and draw its life cycle in the boxes. **Choose a material: plastic, paper, glass or aluminium. Draw the life cycle of ... (the students indicate their choice of material). Draw the raw material in the first box. Draw a factory in the second box. Draw a shop in the third box. Draw people using the goods in the fourth box. Draw a rubbish bin in the fifth box. Draw the recycling symbol in the sixth box.**
FOLLOW-UP 📖 *GREEN ENGLISH DICTIONARY EXTENSION*	Make a poster about the life cycle of different materials. Cut out some pictures from magazines of some objects made of the various materials and match the pictures to the material: Plastic: bottle, toys, ...; Paper: books, newspaper...

WORKSHEET TITLE	**4.4 At the Supermarket**
SPECIFIC AIMS	<u>Communicative functions:</u> expressing possibility. <u>Vocabulary:</u> vocabulary related to shopping (**supermarket, shopping list**), food (**bread, milk, ...**), packaging and storage materials (**non-recyclable materials, paper, glass, plastic, aluminium, composter**). <u>Structures:</u> Wh- questions (**What? Where?**) **Can ....? I/You can ...**
MATERIALS NEEDED	Stationery, pictures of products from the supermarket.
PROCEDURE	1. The teacher asks the students: **What can you buy at the supermarket?** 2. The teacher asks the students to write down what they want to buy at the supermarket on the notebook page on the left side. **Now write your shopping list.** 3. For each product the students have to fill out the chart answering the three questions: **What rubbish do you produce?** **Can you recycle it?** **Where do you put it?**
FOLLOW-UP 📖 *GREEN ENGLISH DICTIONARY EXTENSION* (FACT FILE 14)	Encourage students to think about how they can reduce waste when shopping. Use FACT FILE Eco-shopping.

WORKSHEET TITLE	🎧 4.5 Song: Save Our Planet!
SPECIFIC AIMS	<u>Communicative functions:</u> talking about environmentally-friendly habits, giving orders. <u>Vocabulary:</u> natural elements (**trees, planet**), vocabulary related to the environment (**rubbish, bike**), time expressions (**right now, minute**), feelings (**happy, sad**). <u>Structures:</u> imperative (**clap, start, plant, recycle, ride, do, don't waste**).
MATERIALS NEEDED	Stationery, paper.
PROCEDURE	1. The teacher plays the song (GREEN ENGLISH AUDIO CD - TRACK 19) and asks the students to draw or write what they understand on their piece of paper. **Listen to this song. Draw or write on your piece of paper. Look, like this...** 2. The teacher asks the students what they drew or wrote. **Carmen, what did you draw? What words did you write down?** 3. The teacher tells the students to listen to the song again looking at the words of the song in their worksheets. **Now, listen again. Look at the words on your worksheet.** The students fill in the missing words. **What's missing?** They draw the actions in the boxes. **Now draw the actions in the song. Look, the green ones!** They also draw a sad planet covered with rubbish next to the happy planet. **Now, draw a sad planet.** 4. The students sing the song while miming the actions. They can also be divided up into groups to sing the different verses. **Let's sing the song.** The teacher can also have the students sing using the instrumental version only (TRACK 20).
FOLLOW-UP 📖 *GREEN ENGLISH DICTIONARY EXTENSION*	Invent new verses for the song.

Green English
Environmental Education in English

WORSHEET TITLE	4.6 Make Your Own Paper
SPECIFIC AIMS	<u>Communicative functions</u>: following instructions. <u>Vocabulary</u>: various objects (**bucket, blender, cloth, plastic bowl, clothes hanger, nylon stocking, frame**), materials (**paper**), natural elements (**water, flowers, seeds, leaves**). <u>Structures</u>: imperative (**let's make, tear, put, leave, blend, fill, dip, cover, turn**), prepositions (**in, into, with, over, for**).
MATERIALS NEEDED	Stationery, used paper (preferably printer or notebook paper - newspapers give a greyish colour), bucket, water, blender, cloth, plastic bowl, frame made with a clothes hanger and a nylon stocking.

PROCEDURE	1. The teacher shows the materials in a random order and asks the students to draw them in the boxes.
	Look, this is a blender. Draw the blender in the box.
	
	2. The teacher reads the instructions and the students fill in the blanks with the missing words.
	
	  1. **Tear the paper into small pieces.**
	  2. **Put the pieces of paper in a bucket with water.**
	  3. **Fill the blender with water and paper.**
	  4. **Blend.**
	  5. **Fill a bowl with the pulp. You can add seeds, flowers and leaves.**
	  6. **Make a frame with a clothes hanger and a nylon stocking.**
	  7. **Dip the frame in the bowl and pick up some pulp.**
	  8. **Cover the frame with a piece of cloth.**
	  9. **Turn the frame over and put the cloth in the sun to dry.**
	
	3. The students follow the instructions and make the recycled paper: **Let's make recycled paper.**

FOLLOW-UP 📖 *GREEN ENGLISH DICTIONARY EXTENSION*	The students can make a gift card, a notebook cover or a collage with the recycled paper.

Green English
Environmental Education in English

B

WORKSHEET TITLE	**5.1 Water Water Everywhere**
SPECIFIC AIMS	<u>Communicative functions</u>: expressing needs, talking about percentages. <u>Vocabulary:</u> natural elements (**water, land, world, surface, tree, person, cloud, stones, plants, birds, fish, children, living creatures**), every day objects (**shoes, books, umbrellas**), colours (**blue, brown**), quantity (**percent, numbers up to 100**). <u>Structures:</u> **What...?** Present simple (**cover, need/don't need**), imperative (**colour**).
MATERIALS NEEDED	Stationery.
PROCEDURE	1. The teacher asks the students to colour the water blue and the land brown. **Colour the water blue and the land brown.** 2. The students are encouraged to guess how much water (75%) there is on earth in percentage terms and to complete the sentence in the box. **How much water is there on our planet?** **20%? 90%? 75%?** **Yes, you're right. Water covers 75% of the world's surface.** 3. The teacher shows the picture of the tree, girl and cloud and explains that they are made of a certain percentage of water. The teacher asks the students to colour a percentage of the drawings blue. **60% of a tree is water. Colour 60% of the tree blue.** 4. The students complete the chart with a tick or a check. They write Need / don't need and complete the sentences. **What needs water to live? Do stones need water to live?** **Write "don't need" on the worksheet.** After completing the worksheet, the students think about the conclusions: **Birds are living creatures. They need water.** **Plants are living creatures. They need water.** **What about books? They are not living creatures.** **They don't need water.** **All living creatures need water.**
FOLLOW-UP 📖 *GREEN ENGLISH DICTIONARY EXTENSION*	Students can weigh organic materials that contain a lot of water (a mushroom, orange peel, a piece of apple...) and leave them to dry. After they've dried, they weigh them again and draw conclusions. They write a report on the experiment to put in their Journals.

WORKSHEET TITLE	**5.2 Experiment: Hot and Cold (1)**
SPECIFIC AIMS	<u>Communicative functions</u>: following instructions, expressing the cause and effect relationship. <u>Vocabulary</u>: everyday objects (**saucepan, lid, water, fire**), adjectives (**hot, dry, wet**). <u>Structures</u>: imperative (**put, cover, wait, cook**), verb **can**, prepositions (**in, on, with**).
MATERIALS NEEDED	Stationery, water, heating source (gas stove), saucepan, lid.
PROCEDURE	1. The teacher shows the students the materials in the boxes and asks them to think about what kind of experiment they are about to do. 2. The teacher reads the sentences and asks the students to write them in the right order. **Put the water in the saucepan.** **Put the saucepan on the fire.** **Cover the saucepan with the lid.** **Wait 4-5 minutes and look.** 3. They carry out the instructions. 4. After a few minutes the teacher asks the students to observe the lid. **Is the lid dry or wet? Yes, it is wet.** **Why is it wet? It is wet ... because the fire/heat makes the water evaporate.** 5. The students complete the worksheet by circling the word **wet** and completing the sentence. **This is called EVAPORATION.**
FOLLOW-UP 📖 *GREEN ENGLISH DICTIONARY EXTENSION*	<u>Classroom experiments</u> 1. Put some water in a plastic cup and mark the level of water with a felt tip pen. Leave it in the sun or on a radiator and observe the changes after one day. **Put the cup on the radiator/by the window. Tomorrow we'll check the difference. What do you think will happen?** 2. Let some salt water completely evaporate to observe the salt deposit in the cup/glass.

Green English
Environmental Education in English

B

WORKSHEET TITLE	**5.3 Experiment: Hot and Cold (2)**
SPECIFIC AIMS	<u>Communicative functions:</u> following instructions, expressing the cause and effect relationship. <u>Vocabulary:</u> everyday objects: (**plastic cup, water, marker, freezer, ice, tea, snow**), adjective (**cold**). <u>Structures:</u> imperative (**put, mark, wait, look**), verb **can**.
MATERIALS NEEDED	Stationery, water, a plastic cup, a black felt tip pen, a freezer.
PROCEDURE	1. The teacher shows the students the materials. **Look, what do we need?** The teacher then reads the sentences and asks the students to complete them with the **keywords**. **Put some water in a plastic cup.** **Mark the level of the water with a marker.** **Put the cup in the freezer.** **Wait one hour.** 2. The students do the experiment. 3. After one hour, the teacher asks the students: **What can you see?** The students circle the right answer, ice. **The water has turned to ice.** 4. The teacher has the students observe the level of the ice, noting how the frozen water has expanded. **Now observe the level of the ice: what happened?** **When water freezes it expands.** **This process is called FREEZING.**
FOLLOW-UP 📖 *GREEN ENGLISH DICTIONARY EXTENSION*	<u>Homework</u> The teacher asks the students to try the experiment with other liquids (milk, wine, oil, etc.). They put the liquid in the cup and mark its level and they then freeze it. After a few hours, the students observe what happens and write a report to record their observations to put in their Journals.

Green English
Environmental Education in English

WORKSHEET TITLE	**5.4 The Water Cycle**
SPECIFIC AIMS	<u>Communicative functions:</u> describing facts and processes. <u>Vocabulary:</u> natural elements and phenomena (**sun, sea, vapour, evaporation, clouds, condensation, rain, precipitation, river, collection**). <u>Structures:</u> present simple (**heats up, makes**).
MATERIALS NEEDED	Stationery, cardboard (8 x 40 cm strips, one for each student), scissors, glue, stapler.
PROCEDURE	1. The teacher divides the students into groups/pairs and asks them to try to read the sentences that describe the water cycle. **Read the descriptions. What's missing? Yes, the keywords are missing. Can you guess the words?** 2. The students identify the missing words and draw some simple pictures that describe the various processes. 3. The teacher explains the meanings of the words in the boxes that describe the processes of the water cycle. (**EVAPORATION, CONDENSATION, PRECIPITATION, COLLECTION**). 4. The teacher has the students observe the picture that summarises the water cycle and tells them that this cycle never finishes and is therefore called a never-ending cycle. 5. The students draw and cut out the six phases of the water cycle. They paste them on the strip of cardboard in the right order and they staple the two ends together, forming a hoop. **Draw the sun on a piece of paper.** **Colour it.** **Now draw the vapour / the clouds / the rain / the river / the sea.** **Cut out the drawings.** **Paste them in the correct order on your strip of cardboard.** **Staple the ends to form a hoop.** **Look at your craft: it shows you the never-ending cycle of water.** 6. The students write down the phases of the water cycle in the given boxes and repeat them aloud until they have learnt them, using their craft. They repeat the cycle many times to symbolise the cyclic pattern of the phenomenon.
FOLLOW-UP 📖 *GREEN ENGLISH DICTIONARY EXTENSION*	Brainstorming other cycles (ex. the food chain, recycling ...).

Green English
Environmental Education in English

B

WORKSHEET TITLE	**5.5 Air Pollution Detector**
SPECIFIC AIMS	<u>Communicative functions:</u> describing objects and places. <u>Vocabulary:</u> materials (**cardboard, scissors, string, double-sided sticky tape**), places (**garden, road, classroom, car park**), elements and objects (**hole, tree, window, door**), adjectives (**clean, dirty**), intensifiers (**quite, not very, very, terribly**). <u>Structures:</u> prepositions of place (**in, under, on, near, out of, next to**), imperative (**make, cut, tie, cover**).
MATERIALS NEEDED	Stationery, double-sided sticky tape, cardboard, string.
PROCEDURE	1. The teacher introduces the activity: **Today we are going to investigate air pollution and use an air pollution detector.** **Let's make one!** 2. The teacher asks the students to match the pictures with the sentences. **First, let's reorder the instructions.** **KEY:** **A2, B1, C4, D3.** 3. The students make the pollution detectors following the instructions. **Now let's follow the instructions and make our pollution detectors.** 4. The teacher asks the students to put their pollution detectors in different places, while emphasizing the various prepositions of place. **Mark, put your pollution detector <u>on</u> the radiator.** **Lucy, put your pollution detector <u>under</u> the tree ...** 5. Two weeks later, the teacher has the students collect their pollution detectors and asks them to describe them. **What does your pollution detector look like? What can you see on it? What colour is it? Is it clean or is it dirty? This one is terribly dirty.** 6. The teacher asks the students: **Is the air in the garden polluted?** 7. The students decide which place is the most polluted. **The most polluted place is ... Why? What produces pollution?**
FOLLOW-UP 📖 *GREEN ENGLISH DICTIONARY EXTENSION*	Put the pollution detectors in various places of the home and record observations.

The Organic Kitchen Garden LEVEL B

Green English
Environmental Education in English

WORKSHEET TITLE	**6.1 Growing Vegetables**
SPECIFIC AIMS	<u>Communicative functions:</u> following and giving instructions, expressing needs. <u>Vocabulary:</u> vocabulary related to planting (**kitchen garden, trowel, seeds, watering can, hole, ground, soil**). <u>Structures:</u> imperative (**dig, cover, put, water**).
MATERIALS NEEDED	Stationery, trowel, seeds, watering can, objects which are not necessary for planting (saucepan, ruler, sandwich etc...). The activity should take place in the garden. If it's not possible, it can be done in the classroom with some flowering pots.
PROCEDURE	1. The teacher explains to the students that they are going to plant some seeds and asks them: **What do we need?** Various objects are shown and the teacher asks: **Do we need a saucepan?** **No, of course we don't. What about seeds?** 2. After deciding which objects are necessary, the teacher shows them how to carry out the procedure (either in the garden or classroom) and encourages the students to do the same: **First dig a hole in the ground.** **Now, put a seed in the hole.** **Cover it with soil.** **Water the seed.** 3. After planting the seed, the students go back to the worksheet and match the two parts of the various instructions. **Match the instructions.** Note: This could be also done before planting to familiarize the students with the different stages of planting.
FOLLOW-UP 📖 *GREEN ENGLISH DICTIONARY EXTENSION*	Draw pictures of what the kitchen garden will look like in a week, month, two months...

WORKSHEET TITLE	**6.2 How to Make a Scarecrow**
SPECIFIC AIMS	<u>Communicative functions</u>: identifying parts of the body, following instructions, expressing quantity, asking for and giving personal information. <u>Vocabulary</u>: materials and clothes (**bamboo canes, straw, shirt, hat, buttons, cloth, string**), parts of the body (**eye, head, mouth, ears, arm, leg, body, foot**), numbers. <u>Structures</u>: **What...? How many...?**
MATERIALS NEEDED	Stationery, two bamboo canes (for the 'skeleton'), straw (hair), an old shirt (clothes), an old hat, 8 buttons (2 eyes, 1 nose, 5 mouth), a piece of cloth stuffed with straw (head), string (to tie the various parts together).
PROCEDURE	1. The teacher shows the students the materials and names them. **Look, I've got two bamboo canes, some straw and an old shirt. And here is an old hat, eight buttons, a piece of cloth and some string.** 2. The students match the words to the pictures: **Match the words with the right picture.** 3. The teacher asks the students to guess what they can make with these materials. **What can we make with this? A helicopter? A bicycle? Yes, you're right. It's a scarecrow.** 4. The teacher tells them to fill in the names of the parts of the body and to match them with the various parts of the scarecrow's body. **Complete the words and match.** **KEY: ARM, MOUTH, BODY, EYE, HEAD, LEG** 5. The teacher shows them the materials and asks some questions to help the students understand how to make a scarecrow. **What can we make with bamboo canes? Complete the sentences.** 6. They make the scarecrow and place it in the garden. **Let's make the scarecrow. Let's put it in the garden.** **KEY: 1 arms / legs, 2 hair, 3 old hat / old shirt.**
FOLLOW-UP 📖 *GREEN ENGLISH DICTIONARY EXTENSION*	Scarecrow ID Card, Scarecrow Stories. The students make an ID card for 'Stick the scarecrow' and make up a story about it.

WORKSHEET TITLE	**6.3 The Gardener's Calendar**
SPECIFIC AIMS	Communicative functions: describing actions. Vocabulary: months (**January, February ... December**), vegetables (**artichoke, asparagus, aubergine, beans, beetroot, broad beans, broccoli, Brussels sprouts, cabbage, carrot, cauliflower, chicory / lettuce, courgette, cucumber, endive, fennel, garlic, green beans, leek, onions, peas, potatoes, pumpkin, radish, rocket salad, spinach, sweet pepper, tomatoes**). Structures: **What...?** verb **can**, imperative (**sow, harvest, plan, check, buy, spread, plant, water, weed, clear, protect, put, dig ...**).
MATERIALS NEEDED FACT FILE 20	The FACT FILE **Vegetables: Sowing season and Harvest season** can be used to fill in the boxes. Alternatively, information about the sowing and harvest season of the typical vegetables in specific countries or geographical areas. Stationery.
PROCEDURE	Note: this activity can be done anytime during the year. A record can be made and filled out for each month. 1. The teacher asks: **What can we do in the kitchen garden in January? Can we sow tomatoes?** If students don't know, they can first look at the FACT FILE, or refer to the information they have, and then answer accordingly. **Ok, Things to do in January... This month we can plan our garden ... Write 'Plan our garden' under 'Things to do'.** 2. The teacher helps students write down activities under each month. The procedure is repeated every month. **Things to do** (some ideas): **Plan the garden** **Check the compost** **Sow tomatoes in pots** **Buy seeds** **Spread compost** **Plant onions** **Water plants** **Harvest vegetables** **Weed the garden** **Clear the ground** **Protect plants against pests (use natural remedies)** **Put dead leaves in the compost bin** **Dig the ground.**
FOLLOW-UP *GREEN ENGLISH DICTIONARY EXTENSION*	Ask the students to do a mini survey about the activities that are usually carried out to grow vegetables, take pictures and make a poster. Plan a 'School Kitchen Garden'.

The Organic Kitchen Garden LEVEL B

🌱 **Green English**
Environmental Education in English

WORKSHEET TITLE	**6.4 Pests under Control**
SPECIFIC AIMS	<u>Communicative functions</u>: following instructions, observing cause and effect relationships. <u>Vocabulary</u>: everyday substances (**soap, garlic, beer**), plants (**onions, tomatoes, horseradish, nasturtiums, cabbage, carrots, potatoes, cucumber**), small creatures (**garden slugs, fungi, mosquito larvae, aphids, white flies**), natural remedies (**beer trap, garlic oil, soap spray, herbal repellent - hot and spicy spray**). <u>Structures</u>: imperative (**plant, complete, find**).
MATERIALS NEEDED (FACT FILE 19 - 21)	Stationery, beer, oil, garlic, bar of soap, water, tansy plant, dried lavender flowers, dried or fresh sage, fresh or dried red peppers, plates, bowls, spray bottles, an empty bottle of pesticide (or a photo), FACT FILE **Companion Planting and Pests in the Garden: Natural Remedies**, dead and nibbled leaves.
PROCEDURE	1. The teacher shows the 'sick' leaves to the students and asks: **What can we do for our leaves?** Show the bottle of pesticide and say: **Is it OK to use poisons and chemicals?** The teacher encourages the students to form hypotheses and reminds them: **Our kitchen garden is ORGANIC! We don't use poisons and chemicals. We use natural remedies.** 2. Using the Fact File **Companion Planting**, the teacher explains that some combinations can fix some problems. The students are asked to complete the first part of the worksheet. **Some plants are FRIENDS: they help each other. Look at the picture. What can you see? Can you see the onion and the cabbage? They are friends. Plant ONIONS with CABBAGE to control ... cabbage worms.** 3. The teacher divides the students into groups and hands out the ingredients to each group for making a natural repellent. The students are then asked to look at the FACT FILE **Pests in the Garden** and to follow the instructions: **Now let's make garlic oil.** 4. The students are then brought to the kitchen garden to find plants that have pests. They experiment with the natural remedies. **Can you see garden slugs? Find some aphids in the garden. Let's use Garlic Oil here!**
FOLLOW-UP 📖 *GREEN ENGLISH DICTIONARY EXTENSION*	Make a **'Does it work? Chart'**. After some time, students check the plants that have been treated with natural remedies and record their state of health /health condition. Do a supermarket survey: How many organic vegetables can you find? How much do they cost?

WORKSHEET TITLE	**6.5 How to Make a Salad**
SPECIFIC AIMS	<u>Communicative functions</u>: giving and following a sequence of instructions. <u>Vocabulary</u>: vegetables (**lettuce, cucumbers, tomatoes, carrots**), dressing (**vinegar, salt, oil, pepper**), places (**kitchen, kitchen garden**), colours. <u>Structures</u>: **Where... from?**, Imperative (**wash, peel, slice, pit, dress, enjoy**).
MATERIALS NEEDED	Stationery, tomatoes, cucumbers, lettuce, carrots, oil, vinegar, salt, pepper, knife, salad bowl, forks.
PROCEDURE	1. The teacher asks the students to observe the ingredients and then asks: **Where do tomatoes come from? From the kitchen or from the kitchen garden?** 2. The students write the ingredients under the correct list, either "from the kitchen garden" or "from the kitchen". 3. The students complete the instructions for the salad with the missing words. **KEY:** 1 - **vegetables** 2 - **cucumbers, carrots** 3 - **vegetables** 4 - **vegetables** 5 - **oil, vinegar, salt, pepper** 6 - **salad** 4. The students are divided into groups of 3. One student reads the instructions and the others make the salad. **Now in groups of three, let's make a salad.**
FOLLOW-UP 📖 *GREEN ENGLISH DICTIONARY EXTENSION*	Invent your salad: the students invent and write down recipes for special salads. Ex. The Witch's salad (with spiders, toads, etc.) Friendship salad (ingredients representing love, respect, joy...).

The Pond LEVEL B

Green English
Environmental Education in English

WORKSHEET TITLE	**7.1 Living and Non-living**
SPECIFIC AIMS	<u>Communicative functions:</u> classifying elements. <u>Vocabulary:</u> natural elements/animals (**ground, water, dragonfly, rocks, aquatic plants, turtle, water lily, fish**) **living creatures, non-living things, bottle, shoe, can.** <u>Structures:</u> present simple affirmative and negative **(Don't - eat, reproduce, breathe, grow).**
MATERIALS NEEDED	Stationery.
PROCEDURE	1. The teacher asks the students to observe the picture of the pond and use the keywords to label the different elements in the picture. **KEYWORDS: dragonfly, ground, rocks, turtle, bottle, water, water lily, can, shoe, fish, aquatic plants.** **Observe the picture and look! What can you see in this pond?** **Can you see any animals? Can you see a frog? And a fish? Are there any rocks in the pond?** **Write what you see on the worksheet. What's '***' in English?** 2. The teacher tells them that all things can be classified into living or non-living. **All things can be classified as living or non-living. Remember that living creatures eat, reproduce (have babies), breathe and grow. Non-living things don't eat, don't reproduce, don't breathe and don't grow.** 3. The teacher highlights the differences between a frog and a rock, using gestures to help students understand: **Do frogs eat? Yes, they eat insects. Do they reproduce? Yes, they lay eggs. Do frogs breathe? Do frogs grow? Yes, they do. And rocks? No, they don't. Rocks don't eat. Rocks don't have babies. Rocks don't breathe and they don't grow. A frog is a living thing and a rock is a non-living thing.** 4. The teacher asks the students to analyse the various elements of the pond and to decide if they are living or non-living. The boxes are coloured yellow for living creatures and red for non-living things.
FOLLOW-UP *Green English Dictionary Extension*	Make a poster about the pond or a more general one about the living and non-living world.

WORKSHEET TITLE	**7.2 Food Chains**
SPECIFIC AIMS	<u>Communicative functions</u>: categorizing. <u>Vocabulary</u>: categories (**predators, herbivores, omnivores, microorganisms, decomposers**), animals (frog, **gold fish, grass carp, plankton, annelids, hawk, snake, grasshopper**), general (**pizza, plants, ice-cream, flowers, grass**). <u>Structures</u>: present simple (**be, eat**), **What ...?**
MATERIALS NEEDED	Stationery.
PROCEDURE	1. Students observe the worksheet and brainstorm animals and their nutritional habits. **Look at the frog... What does it eat? Do you think it eats chocolate? Why not? Because it is a...?** 2. The students think of other animals in the categories of predators, herbivores (using common animals like lions, etc)... **Find other predators...** 3. The students complete the worksheet choosing the correct food that different animals eat. **Tick the correct answer. What does a herbivore eat?** **KEY: plants - other animals - everything.** 4. The students complete the sentences at the bottom of the worksheet with their choice of animals and the category the animal falls into. **Complete the sentences.** 5. The teacher shows the students the picture of a food chain. **Look at this food chain. What animal is at the top of the food chain? It's a hawk. What does it eat? Yes, the hawk eats the snake. And the snake? What does the snake eat?**
FOLLOW-UP *GREEN ENGLISH DICTIONARY EXTENSION*	Cut out the pictures in the cut out section and invent other food chains, pasting them in the **Green English Journal**. Possible food chains: aquatic plant - small fish - pike - children - crocodile leaf - snail - blackbird - hawk fly - frog - lizard - cat leaf - rabbit - hawk worm - frog - blackbird - cat fly - frog - snake - hawk. A contest can be held for whoever invents the longest food chain.

WORKSHEET TITLE	🎧 **7.3 A True Story: Frog Life Cycle**
SPECIFIC AIMS	<u>Communicative functions:</u> describing a sequence of actions. <u>Vocabulary:</u> parts of the body (**legs, tail**), vocabulary related to the frog life cycle (**egg, tadpole, frog**). <u>Structures:</u> verb **can**, present simple (**jump, swim, catch, lay, hatch, grow, lose, croak**).
MATERIALS NEEDED	Stationery.
PROCEDURE (FACT FILE 12)	1. The teacher helps the students observe the frog life cycle, paying special attention to the various parts of the picture. **Look at picture number 1. What can you see?** 2. The teacher then plays the CD (GREEN ENGLISH - TRACK 21) and asks the students to complete the sentences using the **keywords**. **KEY:** 4 - **legs** 5 - **legs** 6 - **tail** 7 - **frog** 3. More can be taught about the topic using FACT FILE **Frogs**.
FOLLOW-UP 📖 *GREEN ENGLISH DICTIONARY EXTENSION*	Observation of tadpoles in a container. A frog race: the students pretend to be frogs and have to get to the finish line by following either the teacher's or student's orders: **Jump! Swim! Stop!**

The Pond LEVEL B

Green English
Environmental Education in English

WORKSHEET TITLE	**7.4 Frog Origami**
SPECIFIC AIMS	<u>Communicative functions:</u> giving and following instructions. **<u>Vocabulary:</u>** numbers (1-15), parts of the body (**legs, body, eyes, mouth, tongue**), materials (**paper, glue, scissors**). **<u>Structures:</u>** imperative (**open, turn, fold, cut, colour, paste**).
MATERIALS NEEDED	Stationery, green sheet after worksheet 10.4, paper or cardboard for making the eyes and the tongue. Origami can also be done with coloured cardboard, or by pasting a green sheet of paper onto a sheet of cardboard.
PROCEDURE	1. The teacher shows the students the different steps for making origami (the teacher needs to memorise and practise the steps before the lesson). **First fold the paper like this...** 2. The students follow the steps one at a time by looking at the pictures. **Look at picture number ..., now fold ...** 3. After doing the origami, the students finish the frog by drawing or pasting on the missing parts of the body (eyes and tongue). **What's missing? Where are the legs? And the eyes? Let's make the tongue. Cut the tongue. Paste it in the mouth.**
FOLLOW-UP 📖 *GREEN ENGLISH DICTIONARY EXTENSION*	Make other animals out of origami. For other ideas and suggestions, visit the following websites: http://www.wannalearn.com/Crafts_and_Hobbies/Origami http://www.cybersleuthkids.com/sleuth/Fun_and_Games/Origami/index1.htm/ http://members.aol.com/ukpetd/trad3.htm

WORKSHEET TITLE	**8.1 My Favourite Bug**
SPECIFIC AIMS	<u>Communicative functions</u>: describing an animal. <u>Vocabulary</u>: size (**big, small, medium**), animal body parts (**body, antennae, wings, legs**), actions (**fly, jump, crawl, swim**), places (**pond, house**), prepositions (**on, in**). <u>Structures</u>: present simple (**live, eat, be, have got**).
MATERIALS NEEDED	Stationery, bugs or photos of bugs, magnifying glass.
PROCEDURE (FACT FILES 7 -9)	1. The teacher asks the students to bring a bug to school in an appropriate container that respects the bug's needs. The bugs will later on be freed. Photos can be used as an alternative. 2. The students observe their pet bugs and they draw them in the box. **Observe your pet bug and draw it in the box.** 3. The students fill out the worksheet with the teacher's help. **What's your bug's name? Can it fly? What colour is it? Has it got wings? ...** 4. The teacher asks the students to take turns and introduce their pet bugs to their classmates. Otherwise, they can briefly describe the bugs. **Describe your pet bug.** The other students have to guess the bug. **What is it? Is it a spider?** 5. Butterflies can be chosen to teach more about the topic using the FACT FILES **Insects: Body Parts 2** and **Butterflies and Moths.**
FOLLOW-UP GREEN ENGLISH DICTIONARY EXTENSION (FACT FILE 5)	FACT FILE **Bug Expressions** The students try to understand the meanings of the expressions looking at the pictures **buzz off = go away** **my head is full of cobwebs = I'm confused** **as snug as a bug in rug = cosy and comfortable** **computer bug = problem in the computer** **to open a can of worms = bring up a problem** **snail mail = traditional letter delivery** **I've got butterflies in my tummy = I am nervous and sick** **I'm as busy as a bee = I am very busy** **bookworm = someone who loves books.**

WORKSHEET TITLE	8.2 Spiders and Insects
SPECIFIC AIMS	<u>Communicative functions</u>: describing and comparing. <u>Vocabulary</u>: parts of the body (**wings, antennae, body, head, thorax, abdomen**), bugs (**spider, ladybird, grasshopper**). <u>Structures</u>: **How many...? Have got**, verb **to be**.
MATERIALS NEEDED	Stationery, magnifying glass, a spider and ladybird (or photos).
PROCEDURE	1. The students observe the first part of the worksheet. **Look at your worksheet, it's about insects. Have insects got antennae? How many body parts have they got? How many legs?** 2. The teacher asks the students to observe the spider and ladybird and draw them. **Draw a spider and a ladybird.** 3. The students answer the questions about spiders and ladybirds. 4. The students talk about the differences and complete the text. **Complete the text. Is the spider an insect? And the ladybird?**
FOLLOW-UP 📖 *GREEN ENGLISH DICTIONARY EXTENSION* (FACT FILE 6 - 10)	Use FACT FILES **Insect Body Parts 1** and **Bug Detective**. Sing **'Head and shoulders'** using animal body parts. Comparison between a human body and an animal body. (sung to the traditional tune that can be heard on the internet at http://www.niehs.nih.gov/kids/musich.htm). **Head and body Wings and legs Wings and legs (2 times)** **Abdomen, thorax, antennae and eyes, Head and body Wings and legs Wings and legs.**

WORKSHEET TITLE	🎧 **8.3 A Song: English Country Garden**
SPECIFIC AIMS	<u>Communicative functions:</u> expressing quantity, making lists, asking for and giving information. <u>Vocabulary:</u> animals (**dragonflies, frogs, ants, bees, spiders, butterflies, snakes, fish, worms, creeping things**), natural elements (**trees, breezes, country, garden**), actions (**climbing, come, go**). <u>Structures:</u> **How many...? There is... / there are ... What's ... in your language?**
MATERIALS NEEDED	Stationery.
PROCEDURE	1. The teacher asks: **What can you see in the pictures?** **(elicit) Are they vegetables? No, they are ...** Students guess and write the word ANIMALS in the empty space. The teacher checks the spelling. **How do you spell 'animals'?** 2. The students guess and write the equivalent of the names of the animals in the song which are highlighted in red. **What's 'dragonfly' in your language?** **KEY:** **Depending on the language.** 3. The class listens to the song (GREEN ENGLISH AUDIO CD - TRACK 22) and mimes the movements that correspond to the text. **Listen to the song. Let's mime it.** The instrumental version (GREEN ENGLISH AUDIO CD - TRACK 23) can be used for the students to sing on their own.
FOLLOW-UP 📖 *GREEN ENGLISH DICTIONARY EXTENSION* (FACT FILE 11)	FACT FILE **Honey Bee.** On the basis of the honey bee ID, students make up other IDs for other bugs.

Green English
Environmental Education in English

WORKSHEET TITLE	**8.4 Pet Snails**
SPECIFIC AIMS	<u>Communicative functions:</u> following instructions, asking for and giving information, observing and describing facts. <u>Vocabulary:</u> objects (**aquarium, lid, holes, soil, plants, rocks, lettuce, hamburgers, pizza, obstacle**), adjectives about the weather (**rainy, sunny, snowy**). <u>Structures:</u> **How fast ...?, What kind ...?, What ...?**, present simple (**jump, eat, climb**).
MATERIALS NEEDED	Stationery, aquarium, lid with holes for the aquarium, soil, plants, rocks, lettuce, water, snails (students can find them in the garden), stopwatch (or timer) with a second hand.
PROCEDURE	1. The teacher asks the students what they can make with the materials. They draw the materials in the boxes. **What can we make with these things?** Brainstorming: the teacher writes down these ideas on the board. **Tell me Carla, what can we make?** **Yes, a house for ... ... a zebra? An elephant?** 2. The students try to guess that it is a house for the snails. **Great! ... It's for snails ... for our snails ... our pet snails!!!** 3. The students help to make the house for the snails. **Let's make a house for our snails.** 4. The students have some time to observe the snails and then answer the questions. **How does your snail travel?** A stopwatch or timer can be used to measure the speed of the snail: **How many centimetres in 2 minutes?** 5. They complete the other parts: **What kind of weather do snails prefer?** **What does your snail like to eat?** **What does a snail do in front of an obstacle?**
FOLLOW-UP 📖 *GREEN ENGLISH DICTIONARY EXTENSION*	Suggest keeping a pet snail at home. Try the same activity with another animal.

WORKSHEET TITLE	**9.1 What is it?**
SPECIFIC AIMS	Communicative functions: describing objects. Vocabulary: adjectives (**round, soft, hard, big, small**), objects (related to the adjectives: **melon, rabbit, rock, elephant, ant**). Structures: **What is it? / It's ...**
MATERIALS NEEDED	Stationery, a space outside and natural elements.
PROCEDURE	1. The teacher tells the students that '**I spy ...**' is a traditional English game for kids. **"I spy" is a traditional English game.** A player describes an object with adjectives and the others have to guess what it is. 2. The teacher points to the melon on the worksheet and says with gestures: **This is a melon, it's round. Go and find something round (in the garden). Ready, steady, go!** 3. The procedure is repeated with the other adjectives (see *worksheet 9.2*). The students draw the objects that they have found and they complete the sentences with the teacher's help.
FOLLOW-UP 📖 *GREEN ENGLISH DICTIONARY EXTENSION*	'**I spy**' can be played with other objects that have other shapes, colours and sizes.

See, Smell, Touch LEVEL B

Green English
Environmental Education in English

WORKSHEET TITLE	**9.2 Opposites**
SPECIFIC AIMS	<u>Communicative functions</u>: finding objects with certain characteristics, classifying. <u>Vocabulary</u>: natural elements (**leaf, flower, fishbone, snow, stone, beach, people, fire**), animals (**rabbit, elephant, ant**), adjectives (**soft/hard, prickly/smooth, big/small, smelly/scented, cold/hot, quiet/noisy, young/old**). <u>Structures</u>: **What's ...? It's...**
MATERIALS NEEDED	Stationery, objects, natural elements, a prize (ex. plant, flower, a crown made out of leaves). Note: This activity should be done in a garden or park.
PROCEDURE	1. The students look at the pictures. **What can you see in the pictures? What's big? What's cold?** 2. The students match the opposites. **Match the opposites.** 3. The teacher suggests playing a game either in teams or individually. Prizes are given out to the winners. **A game: Touch something soft... Touch something hard...** Repeat the same game with the other adjectives. 4. Treasure hunt: in groups, the students look for 10 objects based on their characteristics and write/draw them on a piece of paper, which is later added to the Journal. **Go and find 10 things in the garden. Something big, something small, something nice... Then draw them on a piece of paper.** The teacher gives out prizes to the winners. **The winner is ...**
FOLLOW-UP 📖 *GREEN ENGLISH DICTIONARY EXTENSION*	Team game: one team says an adjective and the other team has to say the opposite adjective.

WORKSHEET TITLE	**9.3 Sounds from the Garden**
SPECIFIC AIMS	<u>Communicative functions:</u> likes and dislikes. <u>Vocabulary:</u> animals and natural elements (**birds, dog, cat, duck, insects, wind**), transport (**traffic, car, motorbike**), onomatopoeia and animal sounds (**vroom, bang, crash, woof, tweet, beep, meow, splash, knock, roar, bong, hiss, buzz, cluck, slurp, zoom, thump, pop, splash, crunch, puff, flash**). <u>Structures:</u> **I like / I don't like, verb can.**
MATERIALS NEEDED	Stationery, space outside (or open windows), CD.
PROCEDURE	1. The teacher asks the student to sit down outside in the garden and to be quiet and listen to the sounds. **Sit down and be very quiet. Listen...** 2. The teacher asks them to draw what they hear, separating the sounds they like from those they don't like. **Draw what you hear and separate the sounds you like and the sounds you don't like.** 3. The students answer the questions. **Can you hear the birds singing? Can you hear the traffic? Can you hear cars? Can you hear a motorbike?** 4. The teacher plays the onomatopoeia words on the CD (TRACK 34) and encourages the students to think about how certain sounds can be interpreted differently in two different languages, giving some examples. The students are asked to find other differences. **Ask the students to bring comic books to find some other examples of onomatopoeia.** 5. The teacher says a word and the students have to say the sound for it. For example, car - Vroom vroom / Door - knock knock.
FOLLOW-UP *GREEN ENGLISH DICTIONARY EXTENSION*	Examples of onomatopoeia: *vroom, bang, crash, woof, tweet, beep, miaow, splash, knock, roar, bong, hiss, buzz, cluck, slurp, zoom thump, pop, splash, crunch, puff, flash, woof, slurp, clap, tick tock, drip, scratch, clippety-clop, cock-a-doodle-do, flip-flop, fizz, cuckoo, ding dong, boom, beep, rip, boo-hoo, choo-choo, bow-wow, argh, ouch, belch, blab, blare, bleat, thud, screech, bark, abuzz, bleep, bray, crack, creak, croak, crow, murmur, pit-pat, sob, spatter, splutter, squeak, varoom, clickety clack, yippity yap, clink, clank, woof, crash, munch, hic, purr, meow, burp, hiss, squeal, screech, crackle, zowie, rustling, click, clack.*

Green English
Environmental Education in English

WORKSHEET TITLE	**9.4 Pesto Sauce**
SPECIFIC AIMS	<u>Communicative functions:</u> following instructions, expressing quantity. <u>Vocabulary:</u> ingredients (**basil, Pecorino cheese, Parmesan cheese, cloves of garlic, olive oil, pine nuts**), utensils (**cups, tablespoon, teaspoon, mortar, bowl, jar**). <u>Structures:</u> imperative (**wash, dry, crush, put, add, take, enjoy**).
MATERIALS NEEDED	Stationery, small glass jars, basil, olive oil, garlic, salt, pine nuts, Parmesan cheese, Pecorino cheese, two mortars (for two groups), one bowl.
PROCEDURE	1. The students observe the ingredients in the pictures. **Look at the pictures. What can you see?** **Do you like pine nuts?** 2. The students follow the instructions and take turns crushing the ingredients in the mortar. **Put the ingredients in the mortar and crush them.** **Take it in turns.** **Add the cheese and the oil.** 3. After they have finished making the pesto, the students put it in the jars. **Put the pesto in your jar and take it home. Enjoy it!** As an alternative, the students can make some pasta or try the pesto with bread at school.
FOLLOW-UP *GREEN ENGLISH DICTIONARY EXTENSION*	Family Survey: Try to do some other recipes with herbs. The activity can become a multicultural activity if there are students from other countries.

The House in the Country   LEVEL B

Green English
Environmental Education in English

WORKSHEET TITLE	**10.1 Today and Yesterday**
SPECIFIC AIMS	<u>Communicative functions:</u> describing and comparing houses. Vocabulary: household appliances (**Hi-fi system, TV set, computer, electric kettle, microwave, washing machine, dishwasher, vacuum cleaner, heater**), things from the past (**well, horse and cart, fireplace, cauldron, kettle, washbasin, jug, candle, fiddle, book**). Structures: **There is... There isn't ... / There was ... There wasn't.**
MATERIALS NEEDED	Stationery, pictures from magazines.
PROCEDURE	1. The teacher asks the students to look at the two pictures and gives them the vocabulary: **Look at the pictures. Which one is similar to your house? What can you see? Is there a computer in the picture?** 2. The students have to find 10 differences between the modern and old-fashioned house, and they write down the differences. The teacher helps them write out full sentences on their worksheet. **Find ten differences between today and yesterday.** **Today, in my house there is a TV set. In my great-great grandmother's house there wasn't a...** 3. Make a poster showing pictures of houses from today and from the past.
FOLLOW-UP 📖 *GREEN ENGLISH DICTIONARY EXTENSION*	Field trip to a house in the country. The students try to find things from the past, if there are any. Photo exhibit with captions in English.

The House in the Country   LEVEL B

Green English
Environmental Education in English

WORKSHEET TITLE	**10.2 The Flower Garden**
SPECIFIC AIMS	<u>Communicative functions:</u> describing places. <u>Vocabulary:</u> plants, flowers, garden objects (**plant, pot, daffodils, bench, pond, flower bed, hedge, bush, tree, path, table, chairs, swing, slide, shed**), prepositions (**in, on, under, between, next to, in front of...**). <u>Structures:</u> **There is... It's ... What ...? Where...?**
MATERIALS NEEDED	Stationery, scissors, glue.
PROCEDURE	1. The students look at the black and white pictures. **What is it? Is it an airport? Is it a football pitch?** 2. After guessing that it is a picture of a flower garden, the students go to the cut out pages and cut out the pictures. **Go to the cut out page and cut out the pictures.** 3. The students choose the pictures they want and paste them in their own special gardens and colour them in. **Paste the flowers, the pond... and make your own special garden. Colour it.** 4. The student come up with easy sentences to describe their gardens. **Describe your garden.** **Lucia, there's a big tree between the bench and the swing in your garden!**
FOLLOW-UP *GREEN ENGLISH DICTIONARY EXTENSION*	Creation of a flower garden using pictures made by children or pictures cut out from magazines. Make a poster of different kinds of flower gardens.

The House in the Country LEVEL B

Green English
Environmental Education in English

WORKSHEET TITLE	🎧 **10.3 A Song: An English Flower Garden**
SPECIFIC AIMS	<u>Communicative functions</u>: expressing quantity, making lists, asking for and giving information. <u>Vocabulary</u>: different kinds of flowers (**lady's lace, geranium, dandelion, camomile, gentian, clover, buttercups, roses, daisies, forget-me-nots**). <u>Structures</u>: **How many...? There is... / there are... What's ... in your language?**
MATERIALS NEEDED	Stationery, CD, pictures of flowers, English dictionary.
PROCEDURE	1. The teacher asks: **What can you see in the pictures?** **(elicit) Are they animals? They are ...** The students have to guess the word FLOWERS and write it in the empty space. The teacher checks the spelling. 2. The students ask the teacher the meanings of the various flowers in their native language. **What's "geranium" in your language?** **Key** Depending on the language. 3. The students play a memory game. The students turn over the worksheet and ask each other the meanings of the flowers in their native language. **What's 'dandelion' in your language?** 4. The class listens to the song and sings (GREEN ENGLISH AUDIO CD - TRACK 24-25). The students can also be divided into groups and each group sings the song for each different flower.
FOLLOW-UP 📖 *GREEN ENGLISH DICTIONARY EXTENSION* (FACT FILE 17)	Look for flowers in the flower garden. Use FACT FILE **Flowers**. Use the song for a school show. Make flowers out of used materials (egg carton, plastic cups, straws, cloth...)

The House in the Country   LEVEL B

Green English
Environmental Education in English

WORKSHEET TITLE	**10.4 Save Energy at Home**
SPECIFIC AIMS	<u>Communicative functions:</u> describing environmentally friendly habits. **<u>Vocabulary:</u>** vocabulary related to the house and everyday activities (**home, bedroom, bathroom, kitchen, curtains, covers, pyjamas, heating, shower, bath, water, fridge, food, containers, supermarket, water, energy**), seasons (**winter, summer**). <u>Structures:</u> imperative (**close, use, save, turn up, turn off, make, decide, choose**), present continuous (**do, stand, have a shower, wash, close ...**).
MATERIALS NEEDED	Stationery.
PROCEDURE	1. The students look at the pictures of the house to find the good and bad habits. The teacher encourages the students to think about how their daily activities can help save the environment. **What is the boy doing in the kitchen?** **Yes, he's standing in front of the fridge and the door is open. Oh, no. That's terrible...** 2. The students fill in the gaps with the keywords. **Let's read the text. Fill in the gaps with the correct words.** **KEY:** **BATHROOM: water; energy** **BEDROOM: summer; winter** **KITCHEN: save; supermarket** **LIVING ROOM: lights** 3. The students take turns miming the different situations. The others have to guess. **You're in the bedroom and it's very hot. You are closing the curtains...** 4. The students cut out the sentences from the cut outs and they paste them in the right space. **KEY:** **BATHROOM: Turn the water off when you brush your teeth.** **BEDROOM: Save energy, don't turn up the heating.** **KITCHEN: Decide what you want before you open it.** **LIVING ROOM: Switch off the TV if you are not watching it.**
FOLLOW-UP 📖 *GREEN ENGLISH DICTIONARY EXTENSION* (FACT FILE 1)	FACT FILE **Help the Environment.**

Green English - Classroom Language

Track 56
Saying Hello
Good morning
Good afternoon
Good evening!
Hello / Hi
How are you?
Is everybody here?

Track 57
Let's start
Are you ready to start?
What do we need today?
Have we got everything?
Where is your worksheet?
Have you got a pencil?
What about the clipboards?
Where are they?
First write the date on your worksheet.
What day is it today?
Is it Monday?
Yes, it's Monday the 25th of March.
What's the weather like today?
Is it sunny?
Is it warm?
Let's go out in the garden.
Let's sit down on the bench under the tree.
Today we are going to work in the park!
Today we are going to make recycled paper.
Today we are going to observe leaves.
Today we are going to explore the garden.

Track 58
Working on the task
Work together.
Work in groups.
Work in pairs.
Help your friend.
Please be quiet!
Now listen/Listen carefully.
Be careful … don't touch the stinging nettle!
Respect nature and all living creatures.
Don't waste water.
Sit down, please. Stand up, please.
Come here!
Hurry up ! Quickly, please.
Here you are!
Take your worksheet with you.
Now concentrate. Put your hand up.
Has everybody got … a pot?
Circle the correct word.
Colour the picture.
Complete the sentences.
Copy this sentence in your journal.
Cut out the pictures.
Draw a flower on your worksheet.
Draw what you see.
Fill in the gaps.
Find something … big.
Find the keywords/a spider/a flower
Fold the piece of paper like this. Fold it in half.
Guess what will happen…
Let's make a collage/Let's smell the flowers/
Let's observe the frogs…
Listen and repeat/ Repeat after me…
Look at… those spiders.
Now it's your turn.
Observe carefully.
Paste the leaves on the poster.
Please fetch the pots, choose some leaves, pick some flowers…
Read the instructions carefully.
Reorder this sentence.
Staple the parts together
Underline the keywords
What's missing…?

Track 59
Focus on the language
What's "bruco" in English?
What does "proboscis" mean?
How do you say "cavolfiore" in English?
How do you spell "Hymenoptera"?
Can you repeat that, please?
Could you repeat that, please?
Can you say that again, please?
Can I help you?

Track 60
Encouraging
Your journal is really beautiful!
Try again!
Come on.
Give it a try.
Not bad!
That's better!
Good!
That's great!
Well done!
That's right!
That's correct!
You've got it!
You've done it!
Very good!
Excellent!
Super !
Great!
Amazing!

Track 61
Apologizing
Excuse me.
I'm sorry.
Sorry about that.
Sorry I'm late.

Track 62
Ending the lesson
Have you finished?
Has everyone finished?
Stop working now!
Time's up!
It's time to stop!
Put your things away.
It's time to clean up.
Please tidy up the classroom.

Please tidy up the garden!
Put your things in your bag!
Put the rubbish in the right bin.
Collect all your things.
Let's go back inside.

Track 63
Saying goodbye
Goodbye everybody! See you tomorrow!
See you next time!
Bye! See you soon!
Have a good weekend!
Have a good day!

Fact Files

Help the Environment

How to help the environment: a few tips!

KEEP YOUR NEIGHBORHOOD CLEAN

- Pick up the rubbish and put it in the bin.

HELP KEEP THE AIR CLEAN

- Ride your bike or walk to school: car exhaust fumes pollute the air.
- Don't use "unfriendly" aerosols.

RECYCLE CANS, BOTTLES AND PAPER

- Save them at home and school and help your parents recycle them.

SAVE PAPER

- Use both sides of your paper at school and at home.
- Use sponges or washable cloths instead of paper to clean up messes.

HELP SAVE ENERGY

- Turn off the lights when you leave the room and always turn off the TV when you've finished watching it.
- Don't leave the refrigerator door open: get what you want quickly and close the door.

HELP SAVE WATER

- Don't leave the water running while you brush your teeth.

Parts of a Flower

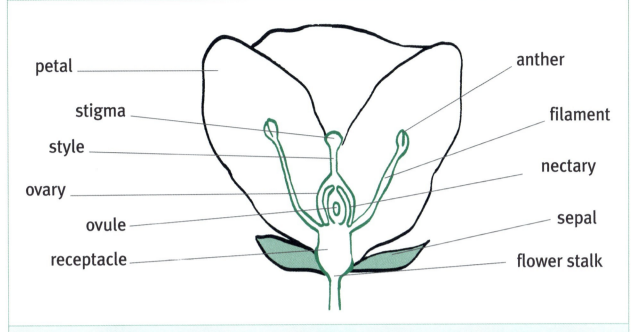

petal

stigma

style

ovary

ovule

receptacle

anther

filament

nectary

sepal

flower stalk

FLOWER PART	PART FUNCTION
Petal	Petals attract insects into the flower
Stigma	It is sticky
Ovary	This will become the fruit.
Ovule	The ovule is like the egg in animals. It will become the seed.
Flower stalk	It supports the flower.
Nectary	This is where nectar is.
Sepal	Sepals protect the flower
Filament	This is the stalk of the anther.
Anther	The anthers contain pollen. Insects collect pollen and transfer it to another flower. The ovule is then fertilised.

The stigma, style, ovary, and ovule = female parts
The filament and the anthers = male parts.

Different Types of Trees

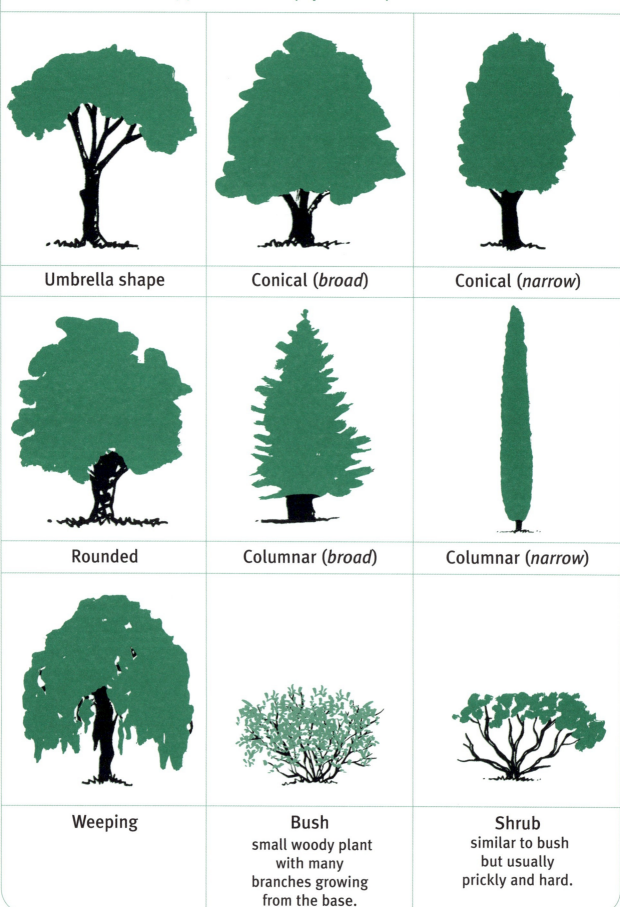

Umbrella shape	Conical (*broad*)	Conical (*narrow*)
Rounded	Columnar (*broad*)	Columnar (*narrow*)
Weeping	**Bush** small woody plant with many branches growing from the base.	**Shrub** similar to bush but usually prickly and hard.

How to Measure a Tree

How to measure the height of a tree:
you will need a pencil, a friend and
a measuring tape.

Choose a tree.
Hold the pencil in a vertical position.
Walk backwards, away from the tree.
Keep your arm straight.
Close one eye and look: when the tree
and the pencil are the same size, STOP.

Now turn the pencil parallel with the
ground.
Keep one end on the edge of the trunk.
Keep your arm straight.
Ask a friend to walk to the side of the
tree until the end of the pencil.
Tell him/her to stop.

Now measure
the distance
from your friend
to the base
of the tree.
This is the height
of the tree.

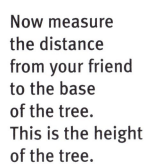

X = height of tree

Bug Expressions

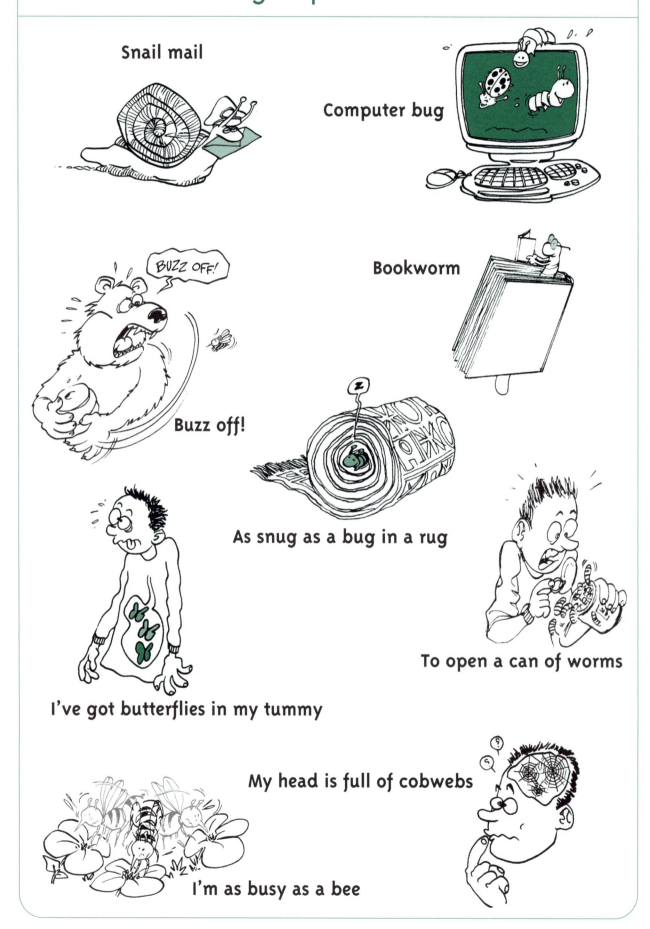

Snail mail

Computer bug

Bookworm

Buzz off!

As snug as a bug in a rug

To open a can of worms

I've got butterflies in my tummy

My head is full of cobwebs

I'm as busy as a bee

Insects: Body Parts 1

Insects do not have bones inside their bodies.
They have a hard outside shell. Insects have six legs and most adult
insects have wings. Insects have three main body parts: head, thorax
and abdomen.

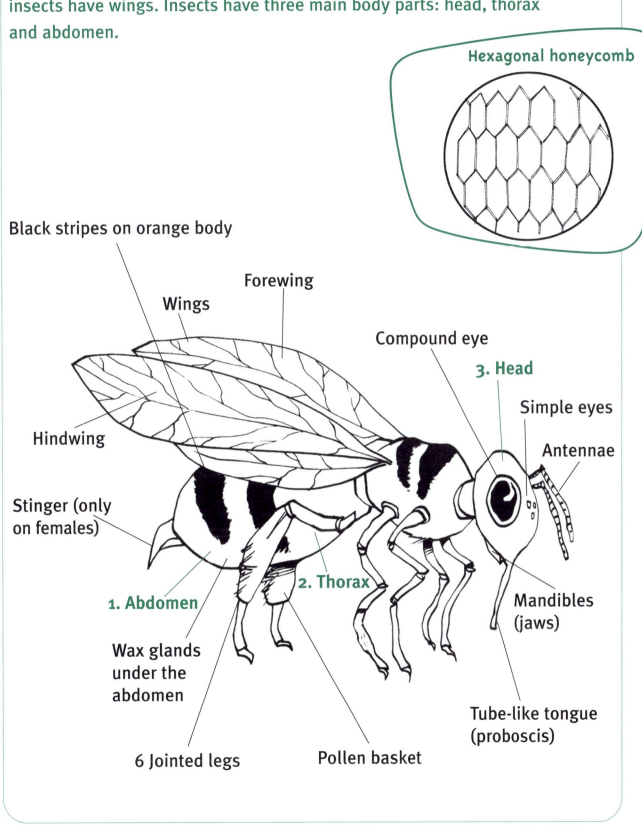

Hexagonal honeycomb

Black stripes on orange body

Wings

Forewing

Compound eye

3. Head

Simple eyes

Antennae

Hindwing

Stinger (only
on females)

Mandibles
(jaws)

1. Abdomen

2. Thorax

Wax glands
under the
abdomen

Tube-like tongue
(proboscis)

6 Jointed legs

Pollen basket

Insects: Body Parts 2

SILKWORM
Bombix mori

Egg

Lemon-yellow at first, then turns black.

White Caterpillar

Thorax   Abdomen

Setae

Head

Silk-producing glands

Ocelli (simple eyes)

Abdominal prolegs

Mandibles (jaws)

Spiracles

Thoracic legs

White Cocoon

White Moth

Feathered antennae

Small white wings

Fat white body

Silkworms

Silkworm moths

Silk is a natural fiber, produced by a moth.
This moth is called *Bombyx mori*. It produces silk.
It cannot fly and moves very little.

Life Cycle

The female moth lays many eggs, and dies.

In the summer, you can see a very little egg.
In the Spring the egg develops and grows.
Then a silkworm comes out!
It is 3 mm and it is hairy.

It crawls around, move its wings rapidly, and mate.

After 2–3 weeks the white moth comes out.

The baby caterpillar eats mulberry leaves.
Silkworms grow very fat!
They can become 6 cm long!

Then they spin beautiful oval cocoons.

Butterflies and Moths

What's the difference between a moth and a butterfly?

Activity

Butterflies are active during the day.

Moths are active at night.

Antenna Shape

Butterflies have club-shaped antennae.

Moths have large feathery antennae.

Food

A butterfly always has a proboscis (tube-like tongue).

A moth does not have a proboscis. Adult moths do not eat. They only eat when they are larvae.

Babies

A butterfly forms a chrysalis. Butterflies do not produce silk.

A moth forms a cocoon, wrapped in silk.

Colours

Butterflies have bright colours.

Moths have dull colours.

Bug Detective ...

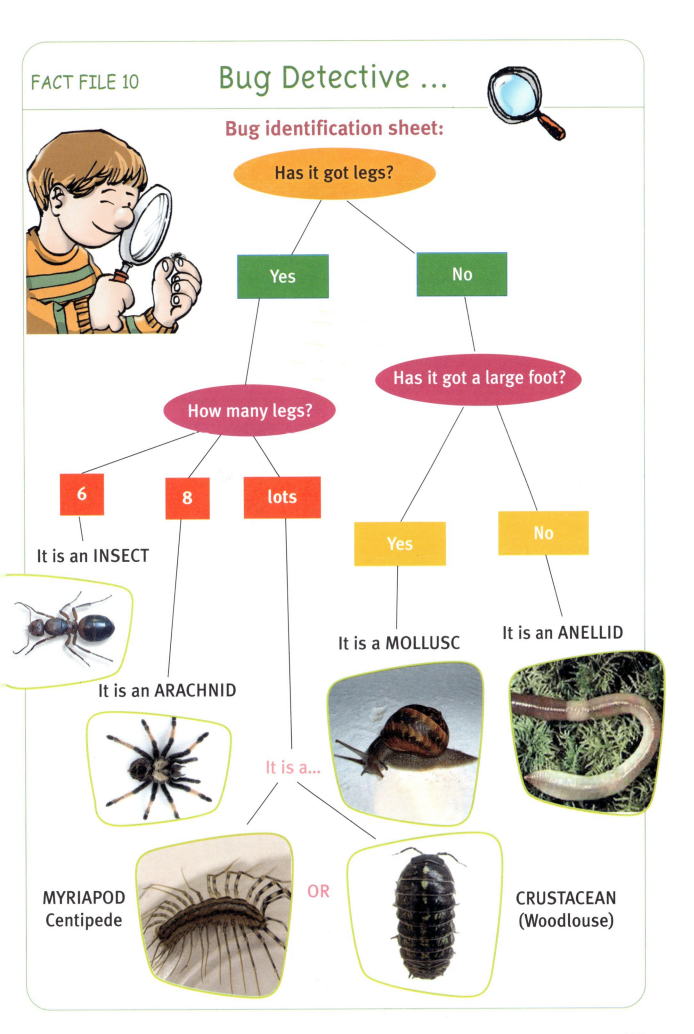

Bug identification sheet:

Has it got legs?

Yes — No

How many legs?

Has it got a large foot?

6 — 8 — lots

It is an INSECT

It is an ARACHNID

Yes — No

It is a MOLLUSC

It is an ANELLID

It is a...

MYRIAPOD
Centipede

OR

CRUSTACEAN
(Woodlouse)

Honey Bee

Name: Honey Bee

Order: Hymenoptera

Description: Bees have hairy bodies and they have pollen baskets on their legs.

Pollen Baskets

Size: 4-25 millimeters

Food: nectar

Home: hives

Other facts: Honey bees take pollen flying from flower to flower, and this helps vegetables and fruit grow.

Honey bees make honey.

Frogs

Frogs are amphibians. They live part of their life in water and the other part on land.

Life Cycle of the Frog

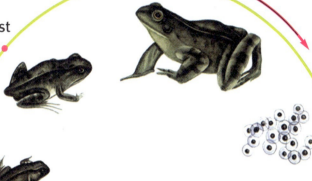

The tail is almost gone.

Eggs are laid in the water and are covered with jelly.

Twelve weeks old: front legs are formed. Tail starts to shrink.

Newly hatched tadpoles.

Eight weeks old: hind legs are formed.

One week old tadpoles.

Six weeks old: external gills disappear.

Young frogs are called tadpoles. They look like little fish. They have a tail and gills.

Adult frogs live on land and breathe air. Frogs have webbed feet for swimming.

Male frogs sing. Some frogs have a vocal sac which fills with air like an amplifier.

Frogs eat insects and small animals like worms and spiders. Frogs have a sticky tongue. Frogs use their tongue to catch insects.

FACT FILE 13 Craft: Make a Bug (with a plastic bottle)

You need: a plastic bottle, cardboard, colours, scissors and sticky tape.

FROG

Body: plastic bottle (cut ✂)
Eyes, mouth, legs: cardboard
(✏ draw and ✂ cut)

DRAGONFLY 2

Body: plastic bottle
Wings, antennae: cardboard
(✏ draw and ✂ cut)

BUTTERFLY

Body: plastic bottle
Wings, head, legs: cardboard
(✏ draw and ✂ cut)

BEE 4

Body: plastic bottle (cut ✂)
Eyes, mouth, legs: cardboard
(✏ draw and ✂ cut)

CATERPILLAR

Body: plastic bottle
Wings, head, legs: cardboard
(✏ draw and ✂ cut)

SPIDER

Body: plastic bottle + dark plastic bag
Wings, head, legs: cardboard
(✏ draw and ✂ cut)

Eco - Shopping!

Eco-shopping helps you to reduce, re-use, recycle.
When you go to the supermarket, remember the environmental impact of packaging! Do you really need that plastic bag?
You can use and re-use a cloth bag!

Shopping list What's in your cart?	What packaging does it produce?	Is the packaging recyclable? ☺ = yes ☹ = no
Corn flakes	Paper / Plastic	☺ / ☺
Crisps	Coupled paper	☹
Egg carton	Cardboard	☺
Detergent bottle	Plastic bottle	☺
Toothpaste	Aluminium tube/ plastic tube	☺
Canned food	Metal can	Find out about your hometown
Mineral water	Plastic bottle	☺
Milk	Tetrapak carton	☹
Meat	Polystyrene tray	☹
Fruit Juice	Tetrapak carton	☹

Leaf Rubbing

How to dry leaves:

If you want to dry leaves quickly you can put them in the microwave oven:
- choose fresh leaves (not fallen leaves)
- place them between two pieces of kitchen paper
- make sure they are flat
- place a plastic tray to press the leaves
- run the microwave oven for 10-15 seconds

Try leaf rubbing with these leaves:

Maple leaf	Bay / Laurel	Ivy	Basswood

Mulberry	Fern	Ash	Oak

With the leaf-rubbing technique you can ...

... make lovely cards ...

... decorate a journal
about a holiday ...

... create a poster for
your bedroom ...

Leaf Classification

Big	Small	Prickly	Hairy
Wide	Slender	Hard	Soft
Oval	Lance-shaped	Simple	Compound
Toothed	Entire	Heart-shaped	Lobed

Other kinds of leaves ...

Needle-shaped
(needles joined at the base)

Needle-shaped
(separate needles)

Compound leaves

Compound-opposite

Compound-alternate

TIPS

KEYWORDS: opposite and alternate

Can you guess what they mean?

OPPOSITE: one in front of the other
ALTERNATE: first on one side and then on the other

Flowers

Tulip

Daffodil

Daisy

Buttercup

Artichoke

Cauliflower

Cyclamen

Snapdragon

Rose

Poppy

Dandelion

Lavender

Thistle

Oleander

Violet

Primrose

Flowers are beautiful decorations, delicious food, excellent medicines.

BUT ... PAY ATTENTION!

Some flowers are toxic: daffodils, buttercups, poppies, oleanders and many others.

FACT FILE 18 Fruit Calendar: Northern hemisphere countries

Fruit ripening season:

	JAN	FEB	MAR	APR	MAY	JUN	JUL	AUG	SEPT	OCT	NOV	DEC
Almond									●	●	●	●
Apple	●	●	●						●	●	●	●
Apricot						●	●	●				
Blackberry							●	●	●			
Blueberry							●	●				
Cherry					●	●						
Chestnut										●	●	●
Fig							●	●	●			
Grapefruit	●	●	●									●
Grapes								●	●			
Hazelnut										●	●	●
Kiwi	●											
Lemon	●	●	●	●								
Melon						●	●	●	●			
Orange	●	●	●	●								●
Peach						●	●	●				
Pear	●	●	●					●	●	●	●	
Persimmon										●	●	●
Plum						●	●	●				
Raspberry						●	●					
Strawberry						●	●	●				
Tangerine	●										●	●
Walnut										●	●	●
Watermelon						●	●	●	●			

Pests in the Garden: Natural Remedies

Ladybirds

Ladybirds, also called lady beetles or ladybugs, are a gardener's best friend.
They eat pests, especially aphids, and their bright colours cheer up the garden.

Herbal repellent

Put tansy, lavender and sage leaves in hot water.
Wait until cold. Spray the plants.

Repels aphids, white flies and other insects.

Soap spray

Put the soap in the water.
Spray the plants.
Repels aphids, white flies and other insects.

Beer trap

Fill a dish with beer.
Leave it near the plants.
Repels garden slugs.

Garlic oil

Put the garlic in the oil and spray the plants.
Use it for fungi and mosquito larvae.

Hot and spicy spray

Put two hot peppers, two cloves of garlic and some soap in the water. Spray the plants.
Repels aphids, white flies and other insects.

FACT FILE 20 Vegetables: Northern hemisphere countries

Sowing and Harvest Season:

	JAN	FEB	MAR	APR	MAY	JUN	JUL	AUG	SEPT	OCT	NOV	DEC
Artichoke			harvest	harvest	sow / harvest							
Asparagus			sow	harvest	harvest							
Aubergine			sow			harvest	harvest	harvest	harvest	harvest		
Beans		sow		sow				harvest	harvest	harvest		
Beetroot				sow	sow / harvest	sow / harvest	sow	sow				
Broad beans				harvest	harvest	harvest				sow	sow	sow
Broccoli	harvest	harvest	harvest	sow / harvest	sow / harvest	sow				harvest	harvest	harvest
Brussels sprouts	harvest	harvest			sow	sow			harvest	harvest	harvest	
Cabbage	harvest	harvest			sow	sow						harvest
Carrot	sow	sow	sow / harvest	harvest	harvest	harvest	harvest	sow / harvest	sow / harvest	sow / harvest		
Cauliflower	harvest	harvest	harvest	harvest	sow / harvest	sow			harvest	harvest	harvest	harvest
Chicory/ Lettuce	harvest	harvest	harvest	harvest				sow	sow	sow / harvest	sow / harvest	harvest
Courgette			sow	sow	sow / harvest	harvest	harvest	harvest	harvest	harvest		
Cucumber			sow			harvest	harvest	harvest	harvest	harvest		

sowing season = 🌱   harvest season = 📦

Vegetables: Northern hemisphere countries

Sowing and Harvest Season:

	JAN	FEB	MAR	APR	MAY	JUN	JUL	AUG	SEPT	OCT	NOV	DEC
Endive			sow		harvest							
Fennel	harvest	harvest	sow / harvest							harvest	harvest	harvest
Garlic	sow	sow		harvest	harvest	harvest				sow	sow	sow
Green beans		sow		sow	harvest	harvest	harvest	harvest	harvest			
Leek	harvest	harvest	sow / harvest	sow	sow	sow				harvest	harvest	harvest
Onions	sow	sow			harvest	harvest			sow			
Peas				harvest	harvest	harvest	harvest			sow	sow	sow
Potatoes	sow	sow	sow							harvest	harvest	harvest
Pumpkin				sow	sow							
Radish			sow	sow	sow	sow	sow	sow				
Rocket salad			sow	sow	sow	sow / harvest	sow / harvest	sow / harvest	harvest			
Spinach	harvest	harvest	harvest	harvest	harvest	harvest				sow / harvest	sow / harvest	harvest
Sweet pepper	sow				sow	harvest	harvest	harvest	harvest	harvest	harvest	harvest
Tomatoes			sow	harvest	harvest	harvest	harvest	harvest	harvest			

sowing season = 🌱   harvest season = 🗃

Companion Planting

Some plants are FRIENDS: they help each other.

Many plants have natural substances in their roots, flowers and leaves that can repel pests.

**Plant ONIONS with CABBAGE
to control cabbage worms.**

**Plant TOMATOES with CARROTS
to control rust flies.**

**Plant NASTURTIUMS with CUCUMBER
to control beetles and bugs.**

**Plant HORSERADISH with POTATOES
to control beetles.**

Companion Planting

More about companion planting to control pests.

INSECT	PLANT THAT REPELS
Ants	Tansy, onions, mint family
Aphids	Chives, garlic, marigolds, mint family, dried and crushed chrysanthemum flowers, coriander, onions, oregano
Cabbage moths	Rosemary, sage, thyme
Cabbage worms	Tomatoes, celery
Carrot flies	Leeks, sage, rosemary
Potato beetles	Green beans, marigolds, nasturtiums, flax
Cucumber beetles	Nasturtiums, radishes, tansy
Flea beetles	Catnip, garlic
Flies	Basil, tansy
Mosquitoes	Basil, garlic, geranium (citrosa)
Onion flies	Garlic
Ticks	Garlic
Tomato worms	Borage
Whiteflies	Marigold, oregano

Favourite veggies (vegetables) and their companions

VEGGIES	FRIENDS	ENEMIES
Beans	carrots, chives, rosemary, sage, radishes, lettuce, cucumbers	onions and fennel
Beetroot	bush beans, lettuce, onions, cabbage	mustard
Cabbage	celery, dill, onions and potatoes	strawberries and tomatoes
Carrots	lettuce, radish, onions and tomatoes	dill
Cucumbers	corn, peas, radishes, beans, carrots and sunflowers	aromatic herbs and potatoes
Lettuce	onions, strawberries, carrots, radishes and cucumbers	lettuce
Onions	lettuce, beets, strawberries and tomatoes	peas and beans
Peas	carrots, cucumbers, corn, turnips, radishes, beans, lettuce	onions and garlic
Tomatoes	carrots, onions, parsley, basil	cabbage, cauliflower, corn, fennel

Green English Audio CD track list

GREEN ENGLISH A

TRACK 1 Copyright
TRACK 2 A story: Drip the Drop
TRACK 3 A song: This Is the Way
TRACK 4 This Is the Way: instrumental version
TRACK 5 A song: Five Little Speckled Frogs
TRACK 6 Five Little Speckled Frogs:
    instrumental version
TRACK 7 A story: Mr Caterpillar

GLOSSARY
TRACK 8 Topic 1: Welcome
TRACK 9 Topic 2: The Orchard
TRACK 10 Topic 3: Plants
TRACK 11 Topic 4: The Three Rs
TRACK 12 Topic 5: Water and Air
TRACK 13 Topic 6: The Organic
    Kitchen Garden
TRACK 14 Topic 7: The Pond
TRACK 15 Topic 8: Bugs
TRACK 16 Topic 9: See, Smell, Touch
TRACK 17 Topic 10: A House in the Country

GREEN ENGLISH B

TRACK 18 A True story: The Plant Cycle
TRACK 19 A song: Save Our planet!!!
TRACK 20 Save Our Planet!!!
    instrumental version
TRACK 21 A True Story: Frog Life Cycle
TRACK 22 A song: English Country Garden
TRACK 23 English Country Garden
    instrumental version
TRACK 24 A song: An English Flower
    Garden
TRACK 25 An English Flower Garden
    instrumental version

GLOSSARY
TRACK 26 Topic 1: Welcome
TRACK 27 Topic 2: The Orchard
TRACK 28 Topic 3: Plants
TRACK 29 Topic 4: The Three Rs

TRACK 30 Topic 5: Water and Air
TRACK 31 Topic 6: The Organic
    Kitchen Garden
TRACK 32 Topic 7: The Pond
TRACK 33 Topic 8: Bugs
TRACK 34 Topic 9: See, Smell, Touch
TRACK 35 Topic 10: A House in the Country

FACT FILES - GLOSSARY

TRACK 36 Help the Environment
TRACK 37 Parts of a Flower
TRACK 38 Different types of Trees
TRACK 39 How to Measure a Tree
TRACK 40 Bug Expressions
TRACK 41 Insects: Body Parts 1
TRACK 42 Insects: Body Parts 2
TRACK 43 Silkworms
TRACK 44 Butterflies and Moths
TRACK 45 Bug Detective
TRACK 46 Honey Bee
TRACK 47 Frogs
TRACK 48 Eco-shopping
TRACK 49 Leaf Rubbing
TRACK 50 Leaf Classification
TRACK 51 Flowers
TRACK 52 Fruit Calendar
TRACK 53 Pests in the Garden
TRACK 54 Vegetables
TRACK 55 Companion Planting

CLASSROOM LANGUAGE

TRACK 56 Saying Hello
TRACK 57 Let's Start
TRACK 58 Working on the Task
TRACK 59 Focus on the Language
TRACK 60 Encouraging
TRACK 61 Apologizing
TRACK 62 Ending the Lesson
TRACK 63 Saying Goodbye

TRACK 64 My Favourite Things

Glossary

A abdomen ....
abdominal proleg ....
absorb ....
add ....
air ....
almond ....
alternate ....
aluminium ....
aluminium foil ....
aluminium tube ....
always ....
amphibian ....
amplifier ....
anchor ....
annelid ....
ant ....
antenna ....
anther ....
aphids ....
apparent ....
edge of the trunk ....
appear ....
apple ....
apricot ....
aquarium ....
aquatic plant ....
arachnid ....
artichoke ....
as snug as a bug in a rug ....
ash ....
asleep ....
asparagus ....
attract ....
aubergine ....
autumn ....

B bag ....
bamboo cane ....
bark ....
base ....
basil ....
basin ....
basswood ....
bauxite ....
bay/laurel ....
bean ....
bee ....
beer trap ....
beetroot ....
beetle ....
bench ....
berry ....
bin ....
bird ....
blackberry ....
blend ....
blender ....
blueberry ....
boil ....
bone ....
bookworm ....

borage ....
bottle ....
bottom ....
branch ....
breathe ....
broad ....
broad bean ....
broccoli ....
brush ....
brussels sprout ....
bubble ....
bucket ....
bulb ....
bush ....
buttercup ....
butterfly ....
button ....
buy ....
buzz off ....

C cabbage ....
cabbage worm ....
calendula ....
camomile ....
canned food ....
car exhaust fumes ....
carbon dioxide ....
cardboard ....
carrot ....
carry ....
caterpillar ....
catnip ....
cauldron ....
cauliflower ....
celery ....
chair ....
chemical ....
cherry ....
chestnut ....
chick ....
chicory/lettuce ....
chimney ....
chives ....
chlorophyll ....
chocolate ....
choose ....
chop ....
chrysalis ....
chrysanthemum ....
cinnamon ....
clean ....
climb ....
cloth ....
clothes hanger ....
cloud ....
clove ....
clove of garlic ....
clover ....
club-shaped antenna ....
cock ....
cocoon ....

cold	....
collect	....
collection	....
columnar	....
compost	....
compost bin	....
composter	....
compound	....
compound eye	....
computer bug	....
condensation	....
conical	....
container	....
coriander	....
coupled paper	....
courgette	....
cover	....
crawl	....
crayon	....
cress seed	....
croak	....
crush	....
crustacean	....
cucumber	....
cup	....
cupboard	....
curtains	....
cut off	....
cut outs	....
cyclamen	....

D
daffodil	....
daily	....
daisy	....
dandelion	....
dark	....
decide	....
decomposer	....
decorate	....
describe	....
destroy	....
detector	....
dig	....
dill	....
dip	....
disappear	....
dish washer	....
donkey	....
double-sided sticky tape	....
dragonfly	....
drain	....
draw	....
duck	....

E
ear	....
earth	....
edge	....
elastic band	....
electric kettle	....
electricity	....
elephant	....
empty	....
endive	....
enough	....

entire	....
environment	....
estimate	....
evaporation	....
expand	....
experiment	....
explore	....

F
factory	....
fall	....
favourite	....
feathered antennae	....
feel	....
felt-tip pen	....
female part	....
fennel	....
fern	....
fertilised	....
fertilizer	....
few	....
fiddle	....
fig	....
filament	....
fill	....
find	....
fireplace	....
flax	....
flower bed	....
flower pot	....
fly	....
fold	....
forget-me-not	....
freezer	....
freezing	....
fresh basil	....
fridge	....
frog spawn	....
fruit juice	....
fruit ripening season	....
fungi	....

G
garden	....
garlic	....
garlic oil	....
gas stove	....
generate	....
gentian	....
gently	....
geranium	....
geranium (citrosa)	....
gill	....
girth	....
gland	....
glucose	....
glue	....
good	....
grapefruit	....
grapes	....
graph	....
grass	....
grass carp	....
grasshopper	....
green bean	....
grow	....
guess	....

H hairy	....		life cycle	....
happen	....		living creature	....
hard	....		lobed	....
harvest	....		logo	....
harvest season	....		lose	....
hatch	....			
hawk	....		**M** magnifying glass	....
hazelnut	....		male part	....
heart-shaped	....		mandible (jaw)	....
heat up	....		manufacture	....
heating	....		maple	....
hedge	....		marigold	....
height	....		marker	....
helpful	....		mate	....
herb	....		materials	....
herbal repellent	....		means of transport	....
herbivore	....		measure	....
hexagonal honeycomb	....		melon	....
hi-fi system	....		mesh	....
high	....		microorganism	....
hive	....		microwave	....
hole	....		milk	....
horse and cart	....		millimetre	....
hot pepper	....		mineral	....
hunt	....		mint	....
hymenoptera	....		mollusc	....
			moon	....
I I'm busy as a bee	....		mortar	....
id (identity)	....		mosquito larva	....
insect	....		moth	....
inside	....		motto	....
insoluble	....		mulberry	....
instruction	....		mustard	....
intrusion	....		my head is full of cobwebs	
ivy	....		myriapod	....
J jar	....		**N** nappies	....
jelly	....		narrow	....
jointed legs	....		natural fibre	....
journal	....		natural remedy	....
jug	....		nature	....
jump	....		nectar	....
			nectary	....
K keep your arm straight	....		need	....
kettle	....		needle-shaped	....
keyword	....		neighbourhood	....
			never	....
L label	....		noisy	....
lady's lace	....		non-organic waste	....
ladybird	....		non-recyclable material	....
lance-shaped	....		nylon stocking	....
land	....			
larva	....		**O** oak	....
lavender	....		observe	....
lay	....		obstacle	....
layer	....		ocelli	....
leaf (pl. leaves)	....		often	....
leave	....		oil	....
leek	....		oleander	....
lemon	....		omnivore	....
lemonade	....		onion	....
length	....		opposite	....
lettuce	....		orange	....
level	....		orchard	....
lid	....		oregano	....

organic waste	....
other	....
oval	....
ovary	....
ovule	....
oxygen	....

P packaging ....

panty-hose	....
paper	....
paper clip	....
parmesan cheese	....
parsley	....
paste	....
path	....
pea	....
peach	....
pear	....
pebble	....
pecorino cheese	....
peel	....
pepper	....
per cent	....
persimmon	....
pesticide	....
pests	....
petal	....
pike	....
pine nut	....
pipe cleaner	....
pollen	....
pollen basket	....
pollute	....
polystyrene tray	....
plankton	....
plastic basin	....
plastic cup	....
plum	....
point	....
poison	....
pond skater	....
poppy	....
popular	....
pot	....
potato	....
pottery	....
precious	....
precipitation	....
predator	....
prickly	....
primrose	....
process	....
produce	....
pumpkin	....
puppet	....
put	....
pyjamas	....

Q quickly ....

quiet	....
quite	....

R radish ....

raspberry	....

raw material	....
receptacle	....
record	....
recyclable	....
recycle	....
reduce	....
refrigerator	....
release	....
remove	....
reorder	....
repel	....
reproduce	....
respect	....
result	....
reuse	....
ribbon	....
rock	....
rocket salad	....
root	....
rose	....
rosemary	....
rounded	....
rub	....
rubbish	....
rust fly	....

S sage ....

sale	....
salt	....
sand	....
saucepan	....
save	....
scarecrow	....
scented	....
scissors	....
screw	....
season	....
seed	....
seedling	....
sepal	....
shady	....
shed	....
sheet	....
shell	....
shoe box	....
shower	....
shrub	....
silk	....
silk-producing gland	....
silkworm	....
simple	....
simple eye	....
size	....
slender	....
slice	....
slide	....
slug	....
small	....
smell	....
smelly	....
smooth	....
snail	....
snail mail	....
snake	....

snapdragon	....
snow	....
soap	....
soap spray	....
soil	....
soluble	....
sow	....
sowing season	....
spawn	....
spicy spray	....
spider	....
spin	....
spinach	....
spiracle	....
sponge	....
spoon	....
spray	....
spring	....
stable	....
stalk	....
staple	....
stapler	....
stem	....
sticky tape	....
stigma	....
stinger	....
stomach ache	....
stone	....
stop	....
straw	....
strawberry	....
string	....
stump	....
style	....
sugar	....
summer	....
sun	....
sunlight	....
surface	....
survey	....
swap	....
sweet pepper	....
swim	....
swing	....

T table ....
tablespoon ....
tadpole ....
tail ....
take in ....
take off ....
tangerine ....
tansy ....
tear ....
teaspoon ....
temperature ....
tetrapack carton ....
thistle ....
thoracic leg ....
thorax ....
throw away ....
tiny ....
to open a can of worms ....
tomato ....

tongue	....
toothed	....
toothpaste	....
touch	....
towel	....
trash	....
travel	....
trowel	....
trunk	....
tube-like tongue proboscis	....
tuber	....
tulip	....
turn	....
turn off	....
turn up	....
turnip	....
turtle	....
tv set	....
twig	....

U umbrella ....
unfriendly ....
Union Jack ....
unscrew ....
usually ....

V vacuum cleaner ....
vegetable ....
vinegar ....
violet ....

W wait ....
walk backwards ....
wall ....
walnut ....
warm ....
washable ....
washbasin ....
washing machine ....
watering can ....
waterlily ....
watermelon ....
wax gland ....
weather ....
webbed feet ....
weeping ....
well ....
wet ....
white fly ....
wide ....
width ....
window-sill ....
wing ....
winter ....
wood ....
woody plant ....
wool ....
world ....
worm ....
wormery ....
wrap ....

Y yucky ....

Bibliography

S. CLARKE, B. SILSBY, *Science*, Sevenoaks, Hodder & Stoughton, 1992

C. BURGESS, *Starting Science*, Huddersfield, Schofield & Sims. Ltd, 1996

J. BRUCE, *Creepy-crawlies*, London, Kingfisher Publications, 2001

S. GODWIN, *A Seed in Need. A first look at the plant cycle*, Have, Macdonald Young Books, 1998

E. L. GRANT WATSON, *What to Look for in Summer*, Loughborough, Wills & Hepworth Ltd, 1960

G. Hall, *Back to Basics Science*, London, Letts Educational, 1996

C. HUMPRIES, *Spotter's Guide to Wild Flowers*, London, Usborne Publishing Ltd, 1978

R. KERROD, *A First Look at Trees*, London, Franklin Watts Ltd, 1972

G. SURDIVALL, *Piccolo Picture Book of Flowers*, London, Franklin Watts Ltd, 1973

Centro Diffusione Lingue Comunitarie, *L'uso veicolare della lingua straniera in apprendimenti non linguistici*, Quaderni USR Piemonte 6, MIUR - Direzione Generale USR Piemonte, Torino, 2003

BARBERO TERESINA, Clegg John, *Programmare percorsi CLIL*, Scuolafacendo, Carrocci Faber. Roma, 2005

Weblinks

www.greenenglish.it

www.archilei.it

www.wwf.org

www.greenpeace.org

www.epa.gov/

www.eeeprojects.net/

www.kidsface.org/

www.kidlink.org/

www.nationalgeographic.com/

school.discovery.com/

www.howstuffworks.com/

www.ecokids.ca/pub/index.cfm

www.kidsdomain.com

www.english-nature.org.uk

www.bbc.co.uk/schools/

www.suggestopoedia.it

www.clilcompendium.com

www.tieclil.org

www.euroclic.net